10 THINGS
SCHOOLS GET
WRONG

AND HOW WE CAN GET THEM RIGHT

DR JARED COONEY HORVATH
& DAVID BOTT

First Published 2020

by John Catt Educational Ltd,
15 Riduna Park, Station Road,
Melton, Woodbridge IP12 1QT

Tel: +44 (0) 1394 389850
Email: enquiries@johncatt.com
Website: www.johncatt.com

ISBN: 978 1 913622 35 0

Set and designed by John Catt Educational Limited

ACCLAIM

'A thoughtful and provocative reflection on the proper aims of education and how they might be achieved.'

Howard Gardner – Hobbs Research Professor of Cognition & Education, Harvard Graduate School of Education; author of *A Synthesizing Mind*

'Horvath and Bott awaken the reader to the importance of questioning the status quo and punch out a compelling solution. This is not more of the same. Rather, it is an original, smart, gritty, honest, and disruptive invitation for educators to think differently – to be better.'

Sir Anthony Seldon – Vice-Chancellor, University of Buckingham; author of *Beyond Happiness*

'*10 Things Schools Get Wrong* is both provoking and consequential. It forces us to rethink some of the most fundamental issues in education. A must-read.'

Yong Zhao – Foundation Distinguished Professor of Education, University of Kansas; author of *What Works Can Hurt*

'This book is full of interesting and novel observations about education. I highly recommend this volume for anyone interested in analysing and improving educational practices.'

Henry L. Roediger III – James S. McDonnell Distinguished University Professor, Washington University in St. Louis; co-author of *Make It Stick*

'This book is for those who know the transformative power of education, but are struggling to convey the changes that need to happen in our schools. Horvath and Bott present a clear vision for change that is both realistic and hopeful.'

Katrina Samson – Head of School, Appleby College

'Sobering and eye-opening. This book makes you wonder what other aspects of schooling we take on faith or continue out of habit. An absolute must-read!'

Catherine Brandon – Director, The Genazzano Institute of Learning & Brain Sciences

'This book balances clarity with nuance. Horvath and Bott treat the reader like s/he is intelligent and offer great food for thought.'

Robert Biswas-Diener – Chairperson for the Working Group on Wellbeing, Global Council on Sustainable Development Goals

'A brilliantly written book about how we might build better, brighter, more purposeful schooling for all young people; and why this matters so, so much.'

Helen Street – Co-Founder & Chair, The Positive Schools Initiative; author of Contextual Wellbeing

'This eloquently written book invites you to step outside the jar and take another look at the art of teaching. The authors take you for an educational ride and make you agree with them: the real experts in teaching are teachers themselves.'

Pasi Sahlberg – Professor of Education, Gonski Institute for Education; author of *Finnish Lessons 3.0* and *Let the Children Play*

'A refreshingly different yet very important book. It is clear the authors have an immense amount of respect for everyone in the teaching profession – powerful and hopeful.'

Kate Jones – Teacher of History, Abu Dhabi; author of *Retrieval Practice: Research and Resources for Every Classroom* and *Love to Teach*

'Honestly – I learned a ton from this book. It offers a fresh take on education informed by a deep understanding of learning and history. Not only is it eye-opening, but it's fun to read as well.'

Jacques-Olivier Perche – Head of Professional Learning, English Schools Foundation; co-editor of *The Big Question in Education*

ABOUT THE AUTHORS

Jared Cooney Horvath

Jared Cooney Horvath (PhD, MEd) is a neuroscientist, educator, best-selling author, and expert in the field of Science of Learning. He has conducted research and lectured at Harvard University, Harvard Medical School, the University of Melbourne, and over 250 schools internationally. He currently serves as Director of LME Global: a team dedicated to bringing the latest brain and behavioural research to teachers, students, and parents alike.

David Bott

David Bott (PGDipEd, PGDipPsych) is the Associate Director of the Institute of Positive Education. As an expert in applied wellbeing science, David has supported thousands of educators from hundreds of schools around the world in designing and implementing system-level approaches to wellbeing. David sits on the Dubai Future Council for Education and has published in academic journals and industry periodicals. He currently serves on the board of the Positive Education Schools Association.

CONTENTS

INTRODUCTION

Education is not broken.

Although this might feel like an odd opening sentence for a book entitled *10 Things Schools Get Wrong*, it's important to recognize that global education is filled with millions of deeply committed teachers successfully guiding the cognitive and emotional growth of hundreds of millions of students every day. Simply because some aspects of a system can be improved, it does not follow that the system as a whole is broken.

Too often, however, educational critics are quick to use imperfection as a rallying cry for complete overhaul. Classrooms getting crowded? Schools have failed us – time for a revolution! Curricula getting outdated? Schools are out of touch – time for a revolution! Pedagogy getting stale? Schools are archaic – time for a revolution!

Let's ignore for a moment that the education system that critics happily malign is by and large the very same system that prepared these critics to write compelling books and deliver engaging TED Talks – the important thing to recognize is that these revolutionary arguments make the mistake of demanding we use a sledgehammer to crack a nut.

In truth, the good produced by schools far outweighs the bad. Globally, more kids have access to education than ever before; more students are graduating than ever before; gender and racial performance gaps are shrinking; bullying is on the decline; student wellbeing has never before been so widely considered; and (for what it's worth) standardized test scores have been consistently increasing for two decades.

Schools are succeeding.

With that said, as the world evolves, so too must certain aspects of education in order to ensure that the greatest number of students undertake the best possible learning. In our estimation, there are 10 pivotal aspects of school that are ready to be evolved and that (if effectively addressed) have the power to produce revolutionary advances in education without the need for a total system overhaul.

Some of these aspects carry the weight of centuries (the 50-minute class period), while others are relatively recent considerations (evidence-based practice). Some have long been questioned by practitioners (grades), while others are hardly recognizable as being open to question (purpose). Some will no doubt ruffle a few feathers (computers), while others will be welcomed by many with open arms (rewards).

In this book, we will dive deeply into these 10 aspects of school and demonstrate not only why each contributes to suboptimal (and potentially harmful) outcomes, but also how each can be adjusted to improve student learning and wellbeing. Importantly, at the end of the book you will find a link to a thorough reference section that can be used to support any argument you wish to explore further.

We'll end this introduction with a quote from astrophysicist Bernhard Haisch:

> *Advances are made by answering questions; discoveries are made by questioning answers.*

With this book, our goal is to pool together robust research and respected philosophy in an attempt to generate potential answers. We hope your goal will be to critically question these answers within your unique context.

Note: Although we have written this book together, from this point forward we will switch our pronoun use to 'I'. We have done this to help ease the reading experience. JCH & DB, November 2020.

CHAPTER 1

EXPERTISE – THE PROBLEM WITH EXPERIENCE

"IN THEORY THERE IS NO DIFFERENCE BETWEEN THEORY AND PRACTICE, WHILE IN PRACTICE THERE IS."
– BENJAMIN BREWSTER

Here are a few interesting observations:

- At the 2019 Australian Institute of Public Accountants Tax Conference, 7 of the 8 featured presenters were practising accountants or tax lawyers. Meanwhile, at the 2019 ASCD Conference on Teaching Excellence, only 1 of the 13 featured presenters was a practising teacher (though 7 were academics).

- At the 2019 Australian Medical Law conference, 8 of the 9 featured presenters were practising medicos or lawyers. Meanwhile, at the 2019 Australian Association for the Teaching of English conference, 0 of the 11 featured presenters were teachers (though 6 were academics).

- At the 2019 Australian Women in Law Enforcement conference, 7 of the 11 featured speakers were practising agents. Meanwhile, at the Australian government sponsored 2019 Beginning Teacher's Conference, 0 of the 7 featured presenters were practising teachers (though 4 were academics).

Do you see a pattern?

Whereas most professional conferences appear to favour inside practitioners who perform the relevant job, teacher professional conferences appear to favour outside academics who talk *about* the job with limited direct experience of the job itself.

Don't misunderstand: I have nothing against academics – I am one and have been so for nearly 15 years. This means I am uniquely poised to point out the following: relying on theorists to drive the practice of teaching is a huge mistake.

The problems begin with perception.

THE FORGOTTEN PROFESSION

Teaching is the only profession that seemingly everyone and their uncle thinks they understand and can perform well:

Those who can do; those who cannot, teach.

This well-worn quote, which characterizes teaching as an innate skill everyone possesses but only the most incapable ever need rely upon, is absurd from both angles.

First, far from being a fallback, nearly 70% of teachers pursue the profession as a first-choice career. Furthermore, nearly 90% of teachers enter the profession as a means to meaningfully impact the lives of children. This suggests that teaching is a true calling for practitioners and not a safety net they revert to only after failing in other careers.

Second, people who 'can do' don't always make for great teachers. Expert blindness is the term used to describe what happens when individuals who attain fluency within a particular field typically struggle to remember what it was like to be a novice, making it difficult for them to effectively guide others. As cognitive psychologist Sian Beilock puts it, 'As you [improve a skill], your ability to communicate your understanding or to help others learn that skill often gets worse and worse.'

I was a student for 12 years – I have a pretty good idea what teachers do.

This strange belief presumes that merely interacting with professionals is sufficient for one to develop deep insight into the relevant profession.

We've all sat through hundreds of films, yet few would presume to comment on what it entails to be a professional actor. We've all gone to dozens of doctor's appointments, yet few would feel qualified to comment on what is required to be a professional physician.

For the most part, we only witness professionals 'performing' a narrow aspect of a far-reaching job. Very rarely do we witness the intense learning, preparation, and practice that goes into achieving mastery. As poet Maya Angelou eloquently puts it, 'We delight in the beauty of the butterfly, but rarely admit the changes it has gone through to achieve that beauty.'

For instance, when it comes to my favourite football team, I only ever watch a 3-hour performance on Sunday afternoon. What I don't see are the countless hours spent training, practising, and strategically planning between each game. Importantly, it's clear that this behind-the-scenes activity is far more relevant to what it means to be a professional than the final public performance.

It is no different with teaching. The 50-minute lessons we all experienced as students were the culmination of countless hours spent learning, planning, preparing, marking, and aligning. Unfortunately, most people never see teachers perform this critical behind-the-scenes work. Needless to say, simply attending class does not offer insight into the profession of teaching any more than listening to records offers insight into the profession of music production.

I am a parent/coach/boss. I teach every day. We are all teachers!

Most people brush their teeth every day which means, at some level, we are all dentists. Nobody makes this argument, however, because it's recognized that dentists perform the act of dental cleaning more effectively and with far more technical knowledge than the average person.

Most people discuss and explore personal issues every day, which means, at some level, we are all psychologists. Nobody makes this argument, however, because clinical psychologists deconstruct life issues more effectively and with far more technical knowledge than the average person.

Most people instruct others every day which means, at some level, we are all teachers. But it's important not to take this argument too far and to recognize that professional teachers instruct students more effectively and with far more technical knowledge than the average person.

Just as the profession of dentistry is more than brushing teeth and the profession of psychology is more than discussing problems, the profession of teaching is more than conveying ideas and information.

Teaching isn't even a real profession.

This is the most pernicious jab against teaching, if for no other reason than because it's frequently made by individuals who carry immense public authority: namely, academics.

Although sociologists continue to debate the precise definition of the term 'profession', most widely accepted characterizations include four criteria. The first three are the need for certification through specialized education, the need for recognized professional organizations at the local, national, or international level, and the need to serve broader social (rather than purely personal) purposes.

Under these three criteria, teaching is most certainly a profession. K–12 teachers must obtain certification via specialized four-year undergraduate or two-year postgraduate education, they have the option of joining any number of selective professional organizations (including the American Federation of Teachers, the Australia College of Educators, and the UK Chartered College of Teaching), and they serve an undeniable social purpose, often with little personal recompense.

However, there is one final criterion that's commonly used to define a profession: <u>professional control</u>. Put simply, this is the ability of practitioners within a profession to internally define, generate, and enforce best practice free from external pressure.

Here's where things get murky.

The sheer number of parties attempting to influence teacher practice is staggering. From politicians to parents to tech developers, it seems everyone has an opinion about how we should define effective teaching. For the most part, teacher professional bodies have done an admirable job of blocking out these external voices to maintain a solid level of professional control amongst practitioners.

Unfortunately, there is one important exception. To understand what it is, let's return to the conference figures listed at the beginning of this chapter. It turns out, those professional bodies that capably fend off external incursions and protect teacher autonomy are the same ones that excessively hire academics to lead teaching conferences, thereby suggesting that the answer to teaching lies outside of teaching itself. This is akin to swatting away flies with your left hand while luring them in with your right: it is a blatant contradiction.

And herein lies the problem of perception. When teachers are seen to rely on outsiders for solutions to insider problems, it not only keeps the door open for non-practitioners to presume they can dictate teaching practice, but it also harms the field's standing as a true profession.

To be fair, this could all be mere vanity. Who cares if teaching is considered a profession? The only thing that truly matters is that the job gets done well.

Unfortunately, the belief that academics can supply the field of teaching with a clear identity leads to an issue far larger than perceived social standing. To understand what this issue is, we need to briefly differentiate between theory and practice.

FROM THEORY TO PRACTICE

Broadly speaking, <u>theory</u> is the realm of scientific explanation. Theory attempts to describe the world by constructing abstracted, idealized, and value-free models.

> *Abstracted*: Scientific theories do not deal in particularities; rather, specific details are often omitted in favour of larger generalizations. Think of road maps – these abstractions omit much detail of the physical terrain in order to simplify the decision-making process for drivers.

> *Idealized*: Scientific theories do not deal in reality; rather, subtle distortions are commonly adopted that reflect nature as it would be in a perfect state. Think of geometry – this idealized branch of maths derives its ratios from perfect circles, triangles, and parallel lines that do not truly exist within the natural world.

> *Value-Free*: Scientific theories do not deal in subjective standards; rather, morals and principles are commonly ignored in favour of impartial observation and measurement. A guiding principle of theory is to describe the world as it *is*, not as it *ought to be*.

Broadly speaking, <u>practice</u> is the realm of physical action. Practice attempts to impact the world by undertaking contextualized, naturalistic, and value-laden activity.

> *Contextualized*: Practice does not deal in abstraction; rather, generalizations are regularly abandoned to account for the unique details specific to a given situation. Think of cooking a meal in a 5-star kitchen versus a college apartment – in both instances the desired outcome is the same, but the specific actions required to achieve this outcome depend upon the particularities of each setting.

Naturalistic: Practice does not deal in idealization; rather, perfect forms must commonly be abandoned in favour of messy reality. Think of kicking a football – although biophysics can describe the 'optimum' kicking motion, in reality kickers must fluidly adjust to variations in weather, air resistance, and terrain in order to attain the desired outcome.

Value-Laden: Practice does not deal in value-free description; rather, nearly every activity is imbued with conceptions of what is good/bad or right/wrong. Think of mowing the lawn – this seemingly innocuous practice is a value-laden activity that reflects beliefs about how a human should interact with nature, the relationship between order and beauty, and the duty of individuals existing within larger social groups.

Importantly, it takes only a moment to recognize that although theory and practice overlap and certainly influence one another, the two are dissociable entities that can (and often do) exist in isolation.

As a simple example, although I understand the mechanics required to juggle (parabolic arcs, gaze fixation, centre of gravity, etc.), I cannot actually juggle! I've tried several times in the past, but have never been able to coordinate my movements well enough to make it work. This means I possess deep theoretical knowledge with little practical knowledge.

Conversely, my 7-year-old niece can effortlessly juggle three balls for minutes on end. Surprisingly, she has no deep understanding of physics, biomechanics, or weight distribution. This means she possesses deep practical knowledge with little theoretical knowledge.

Here's the most important bit: seeing as theories are merely abstracted models meant to describe the world, they cannot in and of themselves alter the world. By all means, an effective theory might influence or inspire practitioners to think differently about their actions, but it can neither dictate nor evolve the characteristics of those actions. As B.F. Skinner states, 'No theory changes what it is a theory about.'

For instance, it's quite possible that theories linking emotion with cognition may influence how a lawyer chooses to try a particular case. However, even armed with this theoretical knowledge, this lawyer must still determine what arguments to make, when to make them, and how to elicit those emotions relevant to winning the case. In the end, although theory may have altered how practice was conceived, it ultimately did not (and could not) determine that practice.

Let's bring this back into the classroom.

PROCESS OF LEARNING vs CRAFT OF TEACHING

Within the field of education, academics deal in theory. By and large, they are dedicated to developing abstracted, idealized, value-free models of *learning*. How does memory work? What role does attention play in perception? How does motivation influence knowledge acquisition? This theoretical work has successfully established that, far from being strictly conceptual, much of learning adheres to predictable neurobiological processes.

Teachers, on the other hand, deal in practice. By and large, they are dedicated to performing contextualized, naturalistic, value-laden activities of *teaching*. What exercises best drive student memory formation? What materials best guide student attention? What routines best support student motivation? This practical work has successfully established a wealth of proven methods for guiding students through the learning process.

Importantly, although the process of learning and the craft of teaching are undoubtedly related, the two pursuits are largely dissociable.

For example, a few months back my neighbour asked how she could help her young son learn how to read. I explained that, within the brain, reading begins as the visual recognition of letters, is followed by the conversion of these letters into auditory sounds, and concludes with the conversion of these sounds into meaning. This means, when teaching a child how to read, it's probably best to start with both visual-letter and auditory-phoneme distinctions, followed by the bolstering of vocabulary to deepen meaning.

After this explanation, my neighbour confusedly looked at me and asked, 'But how do I teach my son letters, phonemes, and vocabulary?' To this, I had no answer.

Later, my neighbour called a mutual friend who is a kindergarten teacher. This friend was able to produce a clear reading plan that included materials like letter blocks, techniques like rhyming, and strategies like word–image matching. Importantly, although this kindergarten teacher has been working in schools for over 30 years, she has never concerned herself with theoretical debates concerning the proposed biological mechanisms of reading.

Let's return one final time to the conference figures that opened this chapter. This data demonstrates that most professional fields maintain a distinction between theory and practice. Although they no doubt draw upon academic thinking, most professional bodies recognize that those individuals best qualified to evolve practice are expert practitioners within the field.

Conversely, within education, theory and practice have been conflated. Today, relevant professional bodies have largely subsumed the craft of teaching under the process of learning.

Again, the argument here is not that theory is useless in education. There is no question that theoretical models like Elaboration, Retrieval Practice, and Spaced Repetition can help teachers conceive of their job in deeper, more constructive terms. The argument is that these theories have little to nothing to say about the actual practice of teaching. What tools should be employed to drive elaboration with nervous Year 1 students? What pacing should be adopted to ensure students who find maths boring will benefit from retrieval practice? What techniques sustain agency when practising spaced repetition with Year 9 boys during a late-afternoon lesson? These are practical issues that can only meaningfully be elucidated and addressed by practitioners of the craft itself.

This means that if we truly wish to advance the teaching profession, we must realign our collective focus to the expert practitioners of this field. But just who might these experts be?

THE NEW EXPERTS

The field of expertise has best been defined (theoretically) by cognitive psychologist Anders Ericsson. Having worked closely with chess grandmasters, Olympic athletes, and high-performing individuals across dozens of fields, Ericsson has dedicated his career to elucidating what constitutes an 'expert' and how expertise is developed.

After 40 years of work, Ericsson has concluded that expertise depends upon mental representations: pre-existing patterns of information held in long-term memory that can be accessed in order to mentally simulate and respond to real-world situations. As a simple example, imagine boiling a pot of pasta.

What signs would there be that the pot is about to boil over and how would you respond to these signs? If you were able to successfully answer those questions, it would be because you have a mental representation for boiling pasta that allows you to recognize and adapt to different pasta-boiling scenarios.

Although everybody uses mental representations, what distinguishes experts from novices is the quantity and quality of these representations. Experts not only have more representations relevant to a particular field, but they also have better organized representations that allow them to respond more effectively and efficiently to ever-evolving conditions. In other words, experts can more effortlessly recognize patterns and adapt to shifting contexts within their domain.

Here's the most important bit: Ericsson has concluded that the only way to develop deep, effective mental representations for a particular field is to undertake explicit, deliberate, and sustained practice within that field. Put simply, it's impossible to develop skill expertise without repeatedly performing that skill.

This means 'expertise' is not a general, all-purpose capability; rather, it is highly contextualized and must be confined to specific domains. This is why there are no expert 'athletes', there are only expert sprinters, hurdlers, or marathoners. This is why there are no expert 'doctors', there are only expert cardiologists, gastroenterologists, and anaesthesiologists.

Returning to education, the only people who have devoted ample time, effort, and energy to the construction of deep mental representations for the craft of teaching are the actual practitioners of the craft. Accordingly, by the very definition of expertise, the only experts in teaching are teachers themselves.

Read that again, because this simple sentence has the power to change many of the dynamics within modern education: *the only experts in teaching are teachers themselves.*

This is the final reason why relying on academics to advance the field of teaching so often falls flat. Aside from the occasional lecture, most academics have little to no practical experience with classroom teaching. Even amongst those academics who began their careers as teachers, the classroom context changes so rapidly that many of their mental models have become outdated and irrelevant to modern circumstances. Furthermore, academics devote their time to developing expertise in the skills of journal searches, data extraction, and theoretical debate. Though valuable in a laboratory, these skills are quite different from those required to expertly guide students through the learning process.

SO NOW THEN...

Once we recognize that teaching is a true profession, and that teachers are the only experts in that profession, three important considerations emerge.

The first concerns teacher training. By some estimates, three-quarters of early-career researchers believe their teaching degree did not sufficiently prepare them for basic aspects of the classroom. In fact, there is increasing evidence to suggest that many teacher training programmes have limited impact on teaching performance and that many school supervisors view recent graduates as unready to adequately perform the job of teaching.

The reason for these findings should now be clear. Most teachers are trained in a university setting by academics who approach teaching theoretically rather than practically. This is as absurd as asking bricklayers to be trained by architectural historians, or chefs to be trained by agricultural chemists. Again, this doesn't mean theory is meaningless; it only means that initial training within any practical field should prioritize *doing* over *knowing*.

With this in mind, it's worth considering how we might adapt pre-service teacher training to focus more on the ever-evolving set of behaviours required to effectively teach. Rather than simply waiting for in-service placement or teaching rounds, perhaps an apprenticeship model could be adopted whereby novice teachers learn the craft by serving as assistants to practising teachers. Or perhaps a practicum model would make sense, whereby teacher training revolves around active role playing or scenario building to help novices develop effective mental representations.

The second consideration concerns expertise. Educational reforms in Western countries often adhere to an 'out with the old, in with the new' mentality. Schemes ranging from the Common School movement to the Teach for Australia programme aim to fast-track teacher training under the belief that fresh ideas and youthful enthusiasm can reinvigorate the field.

If Anders Ericsson is correct and expertise can only accrue via prolonged and deliberate practice of a particular skill, then the most effective teachers will almost certainly be those who have been teaching for some time. In fact, evidence largely suggests that experienced teachers routinely outperform novice teachers, and that new teachers generally require five years of practice before they achieve basic competence. For this reason, reforms that focus on recruitment and the rapid rotation of teachers through the system serve only to ensure that practitioners do not have ample time to develop meaningful expertise.

This is not to suggest that all veteran teachers are strong and all novice teachers are weak. This is merely to reiterate that expertise requires effort and persistence, which means the majority of teaching experts will be found among the ranks of those who have been consciously performing and honing their craft for multiple years. Perhaps rather than being pushed into administrative roles, long-serving teachers could become the apprentice leaders or practicum developers for future teacher training programmes.

The final consideration concerns professional control (i.e. the ability of practitioners within a particular profession to internally define, generate, and enforce best practice). Unfortunately, as discussed previously, as a result of issues of public perception, many external parties are attempting to wrest agency away from teachers.

In order to firmly establish professional control, it's not enough that teachers draw upon each other's experience and expertise to evolve their practice – rather, it's imperative that teachers are *seen* to be doing this in a way that is recognized and respected by the wider public. This requires the creation of a unique <u>body of knowledge</u>: a system whereby knowledge developed in the past is maintained and used to guide knowledge creation in the future.

Lawyers, doctors, scientists, and dozens of other professionals are well respected largely because they have libraries full of material documenting their past and guiding their future. Only after teachers develop a similar system of documentation will they be able to easily fend off and ultimately abate external incursions.

So, what would a teacher body of knowledge entail? That's what the next chapter will explore.

CHAPTER 2

EVIDENCE – THE PROBLEM WITH TRANSLATION

*"WHENEVER YOU HEAR THE TERM EVIDENCE-BASED PRACTICE,
IT'S ALWAYS WORTH ASKING: WHOSE EVIDENCE DO YOU MEAN?"*
– JARED COONEY HORVATH

Before kicking off, it's worth clarifying that whereas in the previous chapter we explored academic theorization (the development of models to describe the learning process), here we are shifting our focus to scientific research (the generation of data to determine which practices most impact student learning). As you will see, although these two concepts are often lumped together, the relevant considerations for each are very different.

Let's tuck in.

Within medical research, there are two classes of experiments: *in vitro* and *in vivo*. In vitro (Latin for 'in glass') denotes experiments that are conducted outside of the body, often with cells or tissue cultures in petri dishes or test tubes. In vivo (Latin for 'in a living thing') denotes experiments that are conducted within living beings.

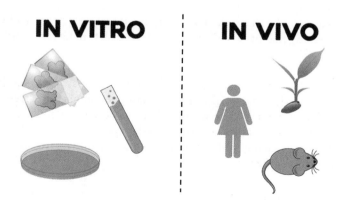

Nearly all newly developed pharmaceuticals begin with in vitro experimentation, as this allows researchers to more easily isolate compounds to determine how they function and interact. Interestingly, of the hundreds of newly developed drug compounds each year that prove effective when tested in vitro, an estimated 90% become either inert or harmful when tested in vivo.

For example, thalidomide was a drug marketed to pregnant women during the late 1950s as a remedy for morning sickness. Unfortunately, when taken during the first trimester of pregnancy, this drug proved to be highly toxic to the developing foetus, leading to an untold number of birth defects and infant deaths around the world.

Following this tragedy, in vitro research was employed to determine that the thalidomide molecule comes in two unique configurations, each an asymmetrical mirror of the other (much like our left and right hands are asymmetrical mirrors of each other). Importantly, this work revealed that only the left-hand form of thalidomide prevents morning sickness, while only the right-hand form causes birth defects. Here, it appears in vitro research has solved a major problem: if we were to develop a purely left-hand version of thalidomide, then we could safely harness the benefits of this drug without adverse side effects.

In fact, drug makers have tried this. Unfortunately, modern (and now mandatory) in vivo drug testing has revealed that as soon as the beneficial left-hand thalidomide molecule enters the human body, it has a 50/50 chance of spontaneously flipping into the toxic right-hand configuration. Although nobody is certain why this sudden shift occurs, it serves as a poignant example of how something that proves effective in a petri dish is not guaranteed to work in the body.

Interestingly, this phenomenon works the other way as well. In the early 1920s, at a time when bacterial infections like pneumonia and streptococcus were often fatal, scientists were working hard to develop effective treatments. The first successfully synthesized antibacterial agent was called Prontosil – a drug credited with saving millions of lives while earning its inventor Gerhard Domagk the Nobel Prize in Medicine.

But here's the twist: Prontosil has no effect in vitro. When Domagk tested this compound against bacteria in a test tube, nothing happened. It was only after he tested Prontosil in vivo (including with his own 6-year-old daughter, who had contracted a severe streptococcal infection from an unsterilized needle) that the antibacterial properties came to light. This serves as a wonderful example of how something that proves effective in the human body might produce no results in a petri dish.

What's going on here? Why is there such a marked disconnect between test tubes and bodies, between cell cultures and people, between the laboratory and real life? And what does any of this have to do with education?

As you've likely noticed, despite more than five decades of intense effort trying to apply scientific research in the classroom, very little tangible impact on teacher practice has been recorded. The sad truth is that, although laboratory data may inspire or influence how educators choose to approach certain situations, it can never directly drive teacher practice.

The reason for this harkens back to why medical researchers must undertake both in vitro and in vivo experimentation if they ever hope to cure disease: prescriptive translation.

EMERGENCE

Within science, prescriptive translation refers to the process of using data or findings generated in one field to guide actions, thoughts, and behaviours in a different field – for example, using findings from biochemistry to drive social epidemiology interventions. Put simply, prescriptive translation seeks to answer the elusive question so many people ask after reading a piece of scientific research: *'What does this mean for me?'*

To understand the process of prescriptive translation, there are two foundational concepts we must first explore.

The first is Levels of Organization. This concept states that when small entities are combined, larger and more complex entities are formed. As a biological example, when many cells are combined, a tissue is formed. When many tissues are combined, an organ is formed. This continues upwards through an organ system, an organism, a population, a community, etc. Put simply, each new level of organization is composed of material from the previous level.

LEVELS OF ORGANIZATION

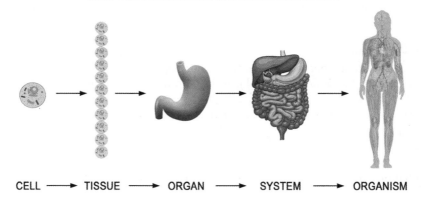

CELL ⟶ TISSUE ⟶ ORGAN ⟶ SYSTEM ⟶ ORGANISM

The second concept we need to understand is <u>Emergence</u>. This concept states that as we move up levels of organization, new properties arise that are neither present nor predictable in earlier levels.

For example, picture a yellow circle sitting alongside a red circle. Now, imagine that you knew everything there was to know about the yellow circle: every yellow molecule, every yellow atom, every yellow particle. In this instance, with absolutely perfect knowledge of yellow, would you have any idea that a colour called orange exists? Of course not, because orange is not *in* yellow.

Now flip it. Imagine you knew everything there was to know about the red circle. Again, with absolutely perfect knowledge of red, would you have any idea that a colour called orange exists? As before, you wouldn't, because orange is not *in* red.

So, where exactly does orange exist? Orange *emerges* only when yellow and red are brought together and allowed to interact. Pull the two apart and orange doesn't split itself evenly among yellow and red – it disappears completely and can no longer be meaningfully discussed. This is the crux of emergence.

Let's return to our earlier example. When many cells combine to form a tissue, valuable properties like permeability, malleability, and mineralization emerge. Importantly, none of these properties exist in any individual cell; they arise only when many cells interact. Similarly, when many tissues combine to form

28

an organ, valuable functions like digestion, circulation, and respiration emerge. Again, none of these functions exist in any individual tissue; they arise only when many tissues interact.

This is why 90% of clinical trials don't survive in vivo testing. When a drug is developed in the lab, it may perform flawlessly on isolated cells or tissues within a petri dish. But, once that same drug is introduced into a larger organism, there's every chance emergent properties will interfere with that performance, triggering unintended and unpredictable consequences (such as left-hand thalidomide spontaneously flipping into a right-hand configuration).

Emergence is why the patterns of an ant colony can never be explained by the make-up and actions of a single ant, why the behaviours of a flock of birds can never be explained by the make-up and actions of a single bird, and why the behaviours of a classroom can never be explained by the make-up and actions of a single student.

FROM THE LABORATORY TO THE CLASSROOM

Within education, the levels of organization we typically draw upon to shape teaching practice are the brain (neuroscience), the individual (psychology), and the group (education). Nothing surprising here.

Problems begin to arise when we are confronted with emergence. More specifically, once a brain comes together with other organs to form a person (i.e. we move from neuroscience to psychology), a number of hugely important properties emerge: movement, behaviour, emotions, consciousness, cognition. Many neuroscientists will never discuss these properties because *they do not exist in the brain*; they only arise when multiple organs interact and can only be meaningfully discussed at the psychological level.

To be fair, behaviours, emotions, and cognitions undoubtedly have neural correlates (regions of the brain that play a role in their emergence). However, this does not mean these properties exist in or are driven by those parts of the brain. This is analogous to recognizing that removing the spark plugs from an engine will cause a car to stop accelerating – but it does not follow that acceleration exists in the spark plugs themselves. Acceleration emerges only via the interaction of many car parts and cannot be reduced to, predicted by, or explained through any single part.

Continuing on, once many people come together to form a social environment (i.e. we move from psychology to education), a number of new properties emerge: communication, relationships, social observation, behavioural mimicry, culture. Again, the reason why psychological researchers have long struggled to coherently explain these phenomena is that *they do not exist in any single individual*; they only arise when many individuals interact, and can only be meaningfully discussed at the educational level.

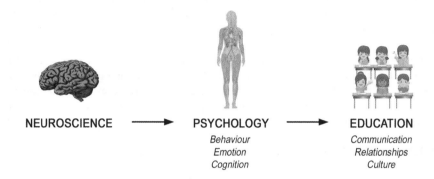

Emergence is the reason why attempts to move neuroscientific or psychological research into schools almost always fall flat. It's not that the data or ideas are wrong – it's that strategies born in a controlled laboratory can never account for the emergent properties that arise in a realistic classroom.

But this hasn't stopped people from trying.

FROM THE ANNALS OF FAILED TRANSLATION

Decades of neuroscientific research have revealed that the brain's primary energy source is glucose, a simple sugar circulated throughout the body via the blood. This means that the human brain is powered almost exclusively by sugar. Accordingly, it stands to reason that if we were to give students more sugar, their brain function and learning would be enhanced.

If this deduction sounds absurd, then someone clearly forgot to tell a prominent, top-100 ranked university in Australia, which in 2016 (on the advice of a well-meaning neuroscientist) spent thousands of dollars ensuring students had ready access to 'brain food' in the guise of jelly beans.

This is a perfect example of the problem with prescriptive translation. It's an incontrovertible fact that the brain runs on glucose and will function quicker when pumped full of sugar. Unfortunately, this does not take into account properties that emerge at ascending levels of organization.

As any parent can attest, once a child consumes sugar, it's not only the brain that kicks into hyper-drive; it's *all* behaviours and cognitions. Attention becomes scattered; movements become dyskinetic; emotions become volatile. Unfortunately, these emergent properties override any benefits that additional glucose may produce in the brain and serve only to hinder learning.

Furthermore, as any teacher can attest, once a dozen kids consume sugar simultaneously, social interactions become chaotic, communication becomes disjointed, and social norms disappear. Once again, emergent properties that are unpredictable by brain research will counteract any learning benefits of increased sugar intake.

Let's move to a possibly more relevant example: *mnemonics*. For over a century, memory-boosting techniques like acronyms, acrostics, and the method of loci have been shown to enhance learning and recall in the laboratory. Therefore, it stands to reason, these techniques should be a mainstay of education.

Unfortunately, countless surveys have shown that mnemonics are rarely used in the classroom and, when they are, they have little to no impact on learning.

Why might this be? Emergent properties, of course.

First, mnemonics take significant time to learn and perfect. Unfortunately, classroom time is limited and, when free time does arise, there are typically far more important things to focus on than memorization techniques. Second, mnemonics appear to only be effective with simple facts or word lists. However, rarely is classroom instruction focused on simple facts or word lists; more often teachers focus on concepts, abstractions, and personalization – material not conducive to mnemonics. Third, memory enhancement using mnemonics appears to fade with time. Luckily, most teachers aren't interested in immediate recall – they're interested in long-term retention and collaborative interrogation.

Again, this does not mean mnemonics are bad or that laboratory research exploring them is wrong. It simply means that this research does not and cannot take into account the emergent properties that arise within a classroom: properties that often overshadow and negate any meaningful impact mnemonics may have.

Intermittent rewards (the brain loves them, but individuals loathe them), forced failure (individuals tend to engage with it, but social groups tend to rebel against it), a water bottle on every desk (although brain slices will die in a petri dish without hydration, no student has ever perished from dehydration in the classroom...though many have started water fights). The list of failed translation due to emergence is unending.

WHAT DO WE DO?

For laboratory research to be meaningfully applied in the classroom, it must first be prescriptively translated. This means ideas born in one level of organization must be redefined, adapted, and retested at each subsequent level. This step-wise movement up the levels of the organization ladder is the only way to account for emergent properties.

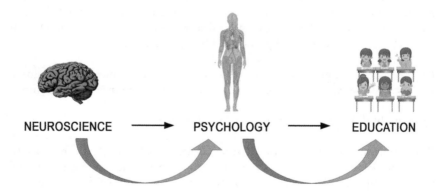

NEUROSCIENCE   ⟶   PSYCHOLOGY   ⟶   EDUCATION

Importantly, this process of prescriptive translation can only be meaningfully undertaken by experts within each relevant level.

For instance, if a neuroscientist wants to apply a specific concept born from biophysics in her laboratory, *it is her job to* redefine that concept using brain-specific language, adapt it to account for brain correlates, and retest the boundaries within her context. Neuroscientists are the only ones qualified to perform this prescriptive translation, as they are the only ones who truly understand and can account for emergent properties within their field. They are the experts.

Similarly, if a psychologist wishes to draw upon neuroscience to drive practice, *it is his job* to redefine, adapt, and retest the boundaries of each relevant concept. Again, psychologists are the only ones qualified to perform this prescriptive translation, as they are the only ones who truly understand emergent properties within their field. They are the experts.

This means, if we ever hope for laboratory research to effectively drive teaching practice, it must first be prescriptively translated by experts within the field of teaching.

But just who are these experts? Chapter 1 should have made this answer abundantly clear.

Nobody in the world understands the decisions teachers must make, the context within which they must make them, or the goals they are trying to achieve by making them. Nobody, that is, except for teachers themselves. Only teachers have devoted the requisite time, effort, and energy to the craft of teaching to effectively recognize and account for the emergent properties that exist within a classroom.

Simply put, for laboratory research to drive educational practice, prescriptive translation must be undertaken by the only people qualified to do it: teachers.

Don't get me wrong – none of this is to suggest that brain or behavioural research is useless. On the contrary, this work can and often does supply teachers with powerful concepts to draw upon for inspiration and ideas. However, the ultimate determination of what these concepts mean for teaching practice can only be derived and established by the practitioners of that craft.

As an example of prescriptive translation in action, let's turn our attention once more to the field of reading.

Recently, neuroscientists discovered that the brain network which processes our 'silent reading voice' is the exact same network that processes any out-loud speaking voice. This means that, within the brain, text and speech interfere. Furthermore, psychologists have long been able to demonstrate that when individuals attempt to read text while listening to aural speech, their comprehension decreases significantly. In other words, the brain interference leads to a clear behavioural manifestation.

Surely, this concept is ready for the classroom, right?

Not so fast. If you think about it, merely knowing that text and speech interfere to adversely impact comprehension does not, in itself, offer any concrete strategies or techniques for teaching. Rather, to make this concept meaningful, teachers must redefine, adapt, and retest this idea within their specific context.

For example, when first learning about text/speech interference, many teachers immediately think to eliminate words from their PowerPoint slides during direct instruction. Although this is a wonderful idea, notice that it's not inherent in either the underlying brain or psychological research; it surfaces only when teachers prescriptively translate the concepts into their unique field. More importantly, the only way to determine if this PowerPoint idea improves student learning is for teachers to test it within their specific context: something neuroscientists and psychologists could never meaningfully do.

Lest I leave you hanging, a number of teachers *have* tested this idea, and removing text from PowerPoint slides does indeed appear to enhance both student learning and participation. However, removing text also leads many students to fear they've missed key content, thereby decreasing short-term learning confidence. These unique findings could only have been derived amidst the emergent properties of a classroom, and whatever additional strategies they inspire amongst teachers can only be developed with a deep knowledge of the craft.

SO NOW THEN...

In summary, as we advance through levels of organization, new properties emerge that are unpredictable and unexplainable by data generated in previous levels. This means, in order for laboratory concepts to be practically useful within the classroom, teachers must prescriptively translate them to their unique context.

Which leaves us with one final issue: evidence-based practice. Over the last decade, there has been an incredible push to make teaching an evidence-based profession. Although this isn't necessarily a bad thing, it does lead to one very important question:

Whose evidence do you mean?

Through this discussion, you've likely come to recognize that evidence is not a singular entity owned and controlled by laboratory researchers; rather, it's a concept that changes and gets redefined across divergent fields. Evidence to a lawyer (e.g. precedent) is very different from evidence to an anthropologist (e.g. stories and myths). Evidence to a neuroscientist (e.g. blood flow) is very different from evidence to a psychologist (e.g. questionnaires). Importantly, none of this evidence is wrong, but it's only meaningful within the context and emergent properties of each relevant field.

This means evidence-based practice within education cannot be defined by practitioners working or data generated outside of the classroom. It must be defined *by* teachers and *for* teachers. Although I can't predict how the profession will ultimately choose to define evidence (qualitative; quantitative; expert judgement; student feedback; etc.), I do know that teachers are the only ones qualified to make this decision.

And herein lies the body of knowledge concept alluded to at the end of the last chapter.

Once it is recognized that research is largely defined by and confined to the field in which it was developed, it becomes clear that teachers must begin to systematically document their attempts at prescriptive translation within the classroom. This does not mean teachers must become scientific researchers; it simply means that teachers must methodically organize and collect information concerning the impact of varied practices within their classroom. This process will generate the evidence needed to push back against unqualified incursions and re-establish professional control amongst teachers.

One final point to consider concerns consistency. Currently, there are millions of teachers working in millions of different classrooms across the globe. With such a massive teaching force, how can we ever expect to achieve any semblance of professional coherence? Here's where it might make sense to steal a page from the book of science.

Scientific research is chaotic. According to several estimations, there are 10 million practising scientists publishing over 2 million research articles per year using thousands of different measures, techniques, and interventions. Despite this, scientific research remains highly integrated and coherent. How? Because all scientific researchers document their work in exactly the same format and they make it accessible in exactly the same repositories. It doesn't matter that researchers all study different (and oftentimes conflicting) things; the simple fact that they can all easily access and decode each other's work allows the entire endeavour to attain coherence without any oversight.

If teachers ever truly hope to build a strong body of knowledge, then it's essential that a consistent means of presenting and disseminating work amongst practitioners is established. It does not matter that every teacher chases different passions, explores different techniques, and works in different classrooms. So long as every teacher's work is consistently organized and made available via a central repository, coherence will emerge without the need for top-down mechanisms.

I'll end this discussion with a quick story.

A while back I joined a state-wide curriculum meeting. Present at this meeting were politicians, lawyers, researchers, and principals. Unfortunately, not a single practising teacher was in attendance. When I pressed the issue, the reason given for the lack of teacher representation concerned the absence of evidence. Every person in that room could point to an entire bookshelf of material that defines the history and current standards of their profession. Unfortunately, teachers cannot do this.

However, through emergence, prescriptive translation, and a consistent framework of documentation and dissemination, teachers can begin to build a reservoir of knowledge unique and relevant to the profession of teaching. Once a body of knowledge has been established and practitioners can unambiguously stand on the shoulders of the past, we will begin to see an evolution of the craft driven by the only people qualified to do it: teachers.

CHAPTER 3

GRADES – THE PROBLEM WITH MODERN ASSESSMENT

"WHEN GALILEO SAID THAT THE LANGUAGE OF NATURE IS WRITTEN IN MATHEMATICS, HE DID NOT MEAN TO INCLUDE HUMAN FEELING OR ACCOMPLISHMENT OR INSIGHT."

– NEIL POSTMAN

Socrates.

One of history's most influential thinkers will forever remain one of history's greatest enigmas. This is because Socrates never wrote anything down. Everything we know about him – from his philosophy to his methods to his death by hemlock – comes exclusively from second-hand sources.

Although historians have been able to use these sources to piece together a fairly complete picture of this man's life, one nagging mystery remains: why was he so averse to writing?

A very compelling explanation can be gleaned from the writing of his most famed student: Plato. In *Phaedrus*, Plato tells the story of Thamus (the king of Egypt) and Thoth (the God of wisdom). In this tale, Thoth presents to Thamus his most beloved of inventions: *writing*. As Plato explains:

> *Thoth declared, 'Writing is a tool, my lord the king, which will improve both the wisdom and memory of the Egyptians. I have discovered a sure receipt for memory and wisdom.'*

Swept up in his own excitement, Thoth must have been shocked when Thamus replied:

> *Thoth, my paragon of inventors... out of fondness for your off-spring you have attributed to it quite the opposite of its real function. Those who acquire the tool of writing will cease to exercise their memory and become forgetful; they will rely on external signs instead of their own internal resources. And*

as for wisdom, your pupils will have the reputation for it without the reality: they will receive a quantity of information without proper instruction, and in consequence be thought very knowledgeable when they are for the most part quite ignorant.

Notice that Thamus was not concerned with what should be written – he did not argue that this tool may be useful for some topics but not for others. Rather, Thamus was concerned with the act of writing – he was arguing that the tool itself required scrutiny.

Herein lies the secret of why Socrates abhorred letters.

VIEW FROM THE TOP

For many decades, neuroscientists conceived of the brain as a passive processor. It was thought that the world entered the body via the senses, these sensations were analysed by the brain, and a largely objective picture of reality emerged. According to this theory, subjectivity is relegated to a relatively late-stage process of interpretation. In other words, human beings all see, hear, taste, smell, and feel the same world – we simply choose to describe things differently.

We now know this conception of the brain is far from accurate.

Rather than passively processing the world, the brain actively predicts how the world *should* be and tunes itself accordingly. This phenomenon is called <u>Top-Down Processing</u>, and it suggests that our expectations feed back to alter our perception.

As a simple example, consider this image:

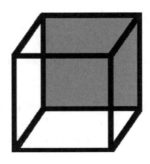

First, imagine the grey square is *solid* and forms the back face of the cube. Next, imagine the grey square is translucent (like a piece of glass) and forms the front face of the cube. Now, begin shifting the grey square at will, alternating it between back and front.

As you're well aware, the image itself never physically changes: the signal entering your brain through your eyes remains constant. However, your expectations for the grey square alter what you see. Importantly, this is not merely a case of late-stage interpretation. Rather, each time you shift your expectations for the grey square, the very first cells in your brain to process vision shift their function in order to alter your direct perception.

In other words, human beings do *not* all see, hear, taste, smell, and feel the same world.

This raises a very important question: where do top-down expectations come from? In neuroscience, it's typically taught that a person's worldview drives his/her top-down expectations. But the astute reader will recognize that this answer only serves to push the question one rung further down the ladder: where, then, do worldviews come from?

As you can probably guess, worldviews are influenced by a number of important sources, ranging from early childhood experiences to education to social interactions. However, there is one incredibly potent source that most people fail to recognize: *our tools.*

Oftentimes we use tools in a blind fashion, without ever thinking about the larger impact they have on our thinking and understanding. However, embedded within each tool is an ideology: a bias that organizes the world in a particular way; that elevates some aspects of reality over others; that redefines common terms; that dictates what can (and cannot) be meaningfully accomplished.

In other words, embedded within each tool is a worldview.

This is what psychologist Abraham Maslow meant when he said, 'To a man with a hammer, everything looks like a nail.' This is what philosopher Marshall McLuhan was alluding to when he said, 'The medium *is* the message.' This is what educator Neil Postman described when he said, 'Tools alter the structure of our interests: the things we think *about*. They alter the character of our symbols: the things we think *with*. And they alter the nature of community: the *arena* in which thoughts develop.'

This is what Socrates (via Thamus) recognized in the story that opened this chapter. He deeply understood that the impact of a tool cannot be judged by how it's employed; it must be judged by how it shifts a culture's worldview. He wasn't worried that writing would make people stupid – he was worried that this tool would redefine 'memory' into something lesser without anyone realizing. He wasn't worried that writing would kill the thirst for knowledge – he worried that this tool would change 'wisdom' to mean the same as 'information' without anyone catching on.

Tools change our reality.

Why does this matter for a chapter exploring school grades?

REIFY, QUANTIFY, RANK

Grading – whether via letters, numbers, percentiles, or smiley faces – is a tool.

Interestingly, we know when and why this tool was invented. In 1792, Cambridge University professor William Farish devised quantitative grading as a means to quickly shuffle students through his class so he could enrol more pupils and earn a larger salary. Little did he know that his simple tool would become globally adopted and precipitate an ideologic shift across the whole of education.

Today, grades are so deeply ingrained within our worldview that most people never stop to consider how bizarre and unnatural the practice of judging a person's thinking on the basis of alphabetic or numeric values truly is. As Neil Postman notes, 'To say that someone should be doing better because he has an IQ of 134, or that someone is a 7.2 on a sensitivity scale, or that this man's essay on the rise of capitalism is an A– and that man's is a C+ would have sounded like gibberish to Galileo or Shakespeare or Thomas Jefferson.'

Because grading is simply a tool, we learn little by asking questions like 'Will students learn better if we employ more nuanced grades?' or 'How can we organize assessment in a way that will improve student outcomes?' The more instructive question to ask is 'What worldview do grades espouse?' In other words, what does the tool of grading *itself* suggest about the world, how it functions, and how it should be approached?

The underlying credo of grading can be summed up in three words: *reify, quantify, rank.*

Reify

Reification is the process of treating an immaterial concept, thought, or idea as a material thing.

For instance, 'beauty' is not a physical object: rather, it is a highly abstract concept used to reference a variety of ever-changing physical, emotional, and mental characteristics. To reify 'beauty', we must define it as something that can be tangibly located and identified in the same manner as the heart, the lungs, or the spleen. When biostatisticians proclaim that 'beauty' is simply the degree of symmetry between the left and right side of a person's face, they have effectively reified this concept.

Why on earth would someone feel the need to reify an abstraction? Because then it can be measured.

Quantify

Once an immaterial concept becomes a concrete thing, we can safely (and seemingly objectively) assign a value to it. For instance, Brad Pitt's face is highly symmetrical, scoring him a 96.7% on the beauty scale. In contrast, Ryan Gosling scores a respectable 73.1%, while Ben Affleck registers a paltry 65.5%.

Why on earth would someone feel the need to quantify a reified abstraction? Because then it can be organized.

Rank

Once an immaterial concept becomes a concrete thing and is assigned a value, we can safely (and seemingly accurately) rank it. In this case, Brad Pitt is more beautiful than Ryan Gosling who, in turn, is more beautiful than Ben Affleck. Importantly, if anyone dares to question this ranking, we can assert that this is not mere opinion – it carries the authority of objective quantification and accurate organization.

Reify. Quantify. Rank.

This is the ideology of grades. In a very real sense, grading and modern assessment espouse a worldview where all human thoughts, skills, and qualities must be reified in order to be considered real, must be quantified in order to be understood, and must be ranked in order to be useful.

PUTTING IT TO THE TEST

To see this rather peculiar worldview in action, let's apply a grading system to 'sophistication'.

As you know, sophistication is not a thing: it's an abstract concept that changes across generations and contexts. In order to assess it, however, our tool demands that we first reify it.

Let us, then, define sophistication as the number of countries a particular person has visited. Now that we've made it a discrete entity, we can locate and measure sophistication within the world. For instance, my 7-year-old niece (who has visited the United States, Canada, and Australia) would score a 3 on the sophistication scale while my 96-year-old grandfather (who has only visited the United States and France) would score a 2. Finally, we can objectively rank everyone according to their final sophistication score.

In the end, what have we really accomplished?

We've asked and answered the question 'Who is the most sophisticated?' in a wholly subjective and restrictive manner. There is no compelling reason to consider sophistication as a by-product of the number of countries a person has visited (which would mean my Year 2 niece would be considered more sophisticated than my veteran grandfather) – but this bias is quickly lost in the measurement.

Once we quantify sophistication, it takes on the feel of an objective measure, and ranking seems both inevitable and accurate. At last we can decide who deserves admittance to selective sophistication programmes, how to organize sophistication support staff, and how to divvy up governmental sophistication funds – all with an air of authority and impartiality.

If this all sounds absurd (and I'm hoping it does), then why do so many of us fail to see this same process at work when we use modern assessment to grade knowledge, understanding, and academic skills? The question 'Who is the smartest?' is no less vapid than 'Who is the most sophisticated?' Yet intelligence has been reified and dressed in the cloak of objective measurement for so long that many people believe we can meaningfully answer the former.

In truth, we've simply allowed the ideology espoused by the tool to permeate our worldview and alter our top-down perception of the world.

What about things like creativity, critical thinking, and collaboration? These 21st century skills are doubtless metaphysical, highly theoretical, and change across contexts and cultures. Surely these deeply human abstractions can never be reified, quantified, and ranked...can they?

- In 2017, Year 6 and 10 students across the state of Victoria, Australia, sat the world's first standardized test of creativity and critical thinking. The results: only 15.3% of students demonstrated peak creativity – a number the Victorian government hopes to increase to 20.8% by the year 2025 via the reallocation of already sparse educational funds.

- As of 2015, schools can purchase CLARA – a simple exam which (employing a mere 5 yes/no questions per construct) can accurately quantify and rank students according to their sense of curiosity, belonging, hope, and five other dimensions. Fortunately, if your students score below 50% on any scale, a paid programme can teach them how to boost their score by more effectively answering those 5 questions.

- Originating in 2008, schools can access Assessment and Teaching of 21st Century Skills – a project which, according to its own description, sets out to 'concretely define in measurable terms high priority understanding and skills'. To believe that we can concretely define (reify) in measurable terms (quantify) high priority understanding and skills is neither a defect of character nor an academic aberration; it is merely indicative of fundamental ideology inherent in assessment.

When you embrace the tool, you must also embrace the worldview.

Don't get me wrong. None of this is to say that some arguments aren't better formulated than others, or that some ideas aren't more agreeable than others. This is simply to say that judging the merit and worth of a thought (and, by extension, the merit and worth of the thinker) using a tool that demands reification, quantification, and ranking is a bizarre practice that is neither intrinsic nor required.

Similarly, none of this is to say that reification, quantification, and ranking did not occur before the invention of the grade. This is merely to say that such an ideology has rarely (if ever) been so deeply embedded within a single tool and so widely adopted in order to define an entire social institution. Grades turned this particular worldview from a part-time curiosity into a full-time requirement.

THE IMPACT OF GRADES ON SCHOOLING

In 2015, the *Washington Post* published an article entitled 'What's the purpose of education in the 21st century?' The answer was perfectly illustrated in the very first sentence:

> *Wisconsin Governor Scott Walker recently tried to change the century-old mission of The University of Wisconsin... by proposing to remove the words in the state code that command the university to 'search for truth' and 'improve the human condition' and replacing them with 'meet the state's workforce needs'.*

As Scott Walker clearly recognized, the process of reification, quantification, and ranking serves little academic or learning purpose. So, what are we ranking students for? The only plausible argument is to ensure universities and businesses can easily sift through candidates in order to identify those best suited for various positions.

If you think this is a bit cynical, I urge you to conduct a simple experiment. Ask 100 people not affiliated with education what the purpose of school is. Chances are that a large proportion will answer something along the lines of 'to ensure students have an opportunity to secure a good career'.

Here's the rub: ask 100 teachers that same question and far fewer will mention anything about helping students get a job.

This means there is a significant disconnect between what educators think the purpose of schooling is and what the public thinks the purpose of schooling is. Though we will explore this issue more deeply in Chapter 10, it's worth mentioning here that this disconnect is largely driven by the tool educators most often employ. When the predominant worldview reads reify–quantify–

rank, then it's easy to understand how education would sacrifice loftier ideals like instilling values and imbuing wisdom in favour of simply teaching students a basic set of marketable skills.

If you (like me) believe school is meant for more than training kids for a good career, then why do we continue to embrace a tool that so clearly signals the exact opposite?

THE IMPACT OF GRADES ON STUDENTS

Narcissus.

According to Greek mythology, this mortal hunter spurned the love offered to him by the god Echo. As punishment, Narcissus was led to a pool of water where he caught sight of his own reflection and fell deeply in love with it. However, upon realizing his reflection was not real and could never truly materialize, he suffered deep despair and committed suicide by falling into the pool of water. His body then rematerialized into the white narcissus flower we see today.

This seemingly straightforward tale is one of the most misunderstood of all Greek myths. It's common for people to interpret this story as cautioning against the dangers of conceit and egocentrism: in other words, vanity cometh before the fall.

But read the myth again. Notice that Narcissus does not fall in love with *himself* – he falls in love with *his reflection*.

This is not a tale of egocentrism. It is a tale about the perils of externalizing one's identity: about favouring public perception over personal understanding. Narcissus falls in love with an unreal image of himself – an image created and reflected back to him by the world. Once he realizes that this reflection is not his true identity, he opts to end his life rather than confront the daunting task of understanding himself, his desires, and his values.

When it's reported that students are increasingly narcissistic, this does not mean they are becoming more self-centred. Rather, it means they are farming out their identity and becoming more dependent upon external validation: as the world says they are, so they must be. This is no better illustrated than in the proliferation of likes, pokes, favourites, thumbs ups, and stars driving an individual's sense of self-worth and accomplishment.

Where on earth might students have learned that external sources are best equipped to accurately determine value, ability, and self-worth?

Reify. Quantify. Rank.

To be fair, human beings have always grappled with the issue of managing outside expectations – but never before have we welcomed externalization to such an all-consuming degree.

For instance, artists have always painted for an audience. However, artists have also traditionally painted for themselves: because they have something to say, not merely because the audience has something they wish to hear.

If you (like me) believe students should strive for more than external validation, then why do we continue to embrace a tool that so clearly encourages the exact opposite?

THE IMPACT OF GRADES ON TEACHERS

When reify-quantify-rank serves as the prevailing ideology, then the practice of teaching becomes nothing more than a set of behaviours that either elevate or diminish rankings. Any technique that raises grades must be standardized and scaled – any technique that lowers grades must be abandoned.

This interpretation of teaching is well illustrated in endeavours like *Visible Learning, High Reliability Schools,* and *The Student Toolbox.* These (and similar) projects aim to systematize teaching by using quantitative research to determine the 'most effective' strategies to boost student learning.

However, an essential point that is often overlooked is what these programmes mean when they say 'student learning'.

As you can likely guess, the data these programmes rely on is heavily dependent upon 'academic outcomes'. In other words, they define improved learning as higher test scores and increased student rankings. Importantly, based on the ideology espoused by grades, this definition of learning is both accurate and effective.

When the craft of teaching is reduced to increasing student rankings, it becomes difficult to see the value of employing human teachers. Surely, an objective computer can adhere to a set of discrete teaching strategies far better than a subjective person.

But what if teaching is about more than increasing student rank? What if teaching is about helping students discover their passions; helping students ask big questions; helping students develop personal agency? When 'academic outcomes' move beyond reification, quantification, and ranking, it becomes difficult to see how blind computers could ever replace conscious human teachers.

If you (like me) believe the craft of teaching is meant to achieve more than improving a student's ranking, then why do we continue to embrace a tool that so clearly promotes the exact opposite?

SO NOW THEN...

There's little doubt that grades will some day go the way of overhead projectors, TV carts, and dot-matrix printers. They do not serve students, teachers, or learning in any meaningful way. Until that day comes, however, how might we best navigate this pernicious tool?

First, although many people conflate grades and assessment, the two are not synonymous. When assessment is used to generate personalized feedback that considers past performance, explicates present performance, and drives future performance, then it can be an incredibly powerful learning tool. Importantly, nowhere in this process need a grade ever appear.

Once numerical values are removed from assessment, then the definition of 'success' becomes more flexible, contextual, and reflective of each student's unique thinking. This is why PhD candidates must perform an oral defence: in this instance, academic supervisors do not make a priori determinations about what they wish to hear, but instead use dialogue to probe deeper into an individual's unique thinking and understanding.

Next, standardized tests have truly embraced the philosophy of grades. They are unashamedly presented as a means of ranking students according to a set of rigid standards. Importantly, in order to rank students effectively, these exams have by and large adapted a binary measurement system whereby every question has a single correct answer. Even seemingly open-ended components, like the writing comprehension section of the SAT exams, are scored according to a strict rubric that defines what words, phrases, and/or ideas must be included for a piece of writing to be considered effective.

Here's the rub: those government, university, and business officials who most publicly demand that teachers embrace standardized tests are typically the same people who decry teachers for 'teaching to the test'. This is akin to denouncing football coaches for teaching to the game or condemning choir directors for teaching to the concert.

If the parameters of a performance are well established and the specific requirements to achieve success have been determined in advance, it would be morally inappropriate to keep students in the dark and simply hope they figure out how to make the transition from learning to performance. When the academic future of children rests on whether or not they can answer a predetermined set of binary questions, then by all means we should explicitly teach them how to answer those questions.

However, whereas it's perfectly reasonable to teach to the test, we shouldn't teach *only* to the test. Fortunately, explicitly teaching test material does not require much time or effort. During my four years of university tutoring, I dedicated only 30 minutes of each class to explicitly covering test material; the remaining 90 minutes were focused on the type of deep, nuanced, non-binary learning that students were far more interested in. Each year, not only did my tutorial students blitz the final exam, but they outperformed other students on the final written and oral assignments as well. In a very real sense, teaching to the test paved the way for teaching *beyond* the test.

Let's conclude with a short story about a small Australian primary school which shall remain nameless (for reasons that will shortly become clear).

For over a decade, this school scored below national averages on standardized exam performance. In 2016, they decided to realign their priorities by focusing strictly on improving student learning. To this end, one of their first moves was eliminating all grades and marks. In fairness, students were still required to take standardized exams (as this is a requirement for government funding), but an agreement was made between the school and parents that students would never be told their results.

In 2019, this school scored in the top quartile of growth across the nation on standardized exam performance. In fact, in only 3 years, their average reading km

scores moved from one standard deviation *below* the national average to one standard deviation *above* the national average.

The reason I don't use the school's name here is because neither the students, teachers, nor parents have any idea this growth has occurred. The principal recognizes that to advertise their standardized test performance would be in direct contradiction of the new school philosophy. They did not abandon grades for the purpose of increasing test scores; that outcome was simply a by-product of elevating learning above ranking.

I tell this story because it well demonstrates that not only is eliminating marks from school a real possibility, but also it need not negatively impact student performance.

CHAPTER 4

HOMEWORK – THE PROBLEM WITH OPPORTUNITY COST

"YOU CAN DO ANYTHING, BUT NOT EVERYTHING."
– DAVID ALLEN

If you ask five plumbers why they install drainpipes with a gradient of at least 1.65%, they'll likely all tell you that this is the minimum safe 'fall' to prevent possible build-up of waste water. If you ask five professional tennis players why they change racquets regularly during matches, they'll likely all tell you that this helps to ensure string tension remains constant. If you ask five teachers why they assign homework, they'll likely all tell you something very different – ranging from providing practice opportunities to flipping classroom learning to engaging parents in the learning process.

Despite the lack of consensus, the popular justifications for assigning homework seem reasonable, logical, and even fundamental. However, many seem to reflect personal preference rather than a robust base of evidence.

In Australia alone, a country with around 10,000 schools, students this year will collectively complete approximately 350 million hours of homework. That's more than 40,000 years' worth of time. This, by the way, is also a country where, according to the Australian Institute of Health and Welfare, over 90% of teenagers fail to meet basic daily physical exercise recommendations (one hour of moderately intense activity).

This is not to suggest that kids should necessarily be running around instead of doing homework (although a compelling argument could be made for this). It is merely to say that with such a massive investment of time and energy, it's reasonable to assume we must have clear answers to questions like: Does homework actually work? Is it effective at improving student learning (and, if so, under what circumstances)? How much homework is ideal? How frequently should it be assigned? For whom is it best suited?

A THOUGHT EXPERIMENT

Let's consider the hypothetical case of Alex and Ben.

Alex and Ben are twin boys. They are 13 years old and they're enrolled in all the same Year 7 classes at the local public high school. It is an excellent school and Alex and Ben are both very dedicated, engaged students.

On Monday, Alex and Ben go to school and enjoy their lessons in science, English, history, art, and mathematics. They work hard and meaningfully contribute to each lesson. In this particular school, the homework guidelines stipulate that each teacher should assign 15 minutes of *optional* homework per lesson; students can choose to complete the homework or not – there are no prizes for completion and no penalties for non-completion.

Alex catches the bus and arrives home from school that day at 4:30 p.m. He has a quick snack and then heads to his room to begin his homework at 5:00 p.m. Independently, he completes his science, English, and maths homework – just in time to join his family for dinner at 6:00 p.m.

After dinner, Alex heads back to his room, where he continues to work until 7:30 p.m. Having completed all his homework, Alex is understandably tired and, although he wishes he had the energy to read, he settles in to watch a few YouTube videos of his favourite basketball players. Alex loves basketball, but often doesn't have the time or energy to practise as much as he'd like. At 8:30 p.m., he gets ready for bed and has the lights out by 9:00 p.m.

Ben, on the other hand, stays after school that day to practise football for an hour with a group of friends. They train rigorously but share lots of laughs, too. After training, Ben catches the bus back to his neighbour's house, where he and two friends regularly meet for band practice. Ben plays the guitar and enjoys creating music in a social environment. After jamming for 45 minutes, Ben heads home just in time to have dinner with Alex and his family.

Following dinner, while Alex completes his homework, Ben and his dad work together to plan their next family camping trip. They want to make it really special, so they discuss various outdoor activities that would be best suited to different camping locations. They research cultural and historical sites that might be interesting to visit, and Ben jots down notes to share with his brother and mum. By 8:00 p.m., the trip is sketched out, so Ben sits with his mum and reads a Harry Potter novel for 30 minutes. At 8:30 p.m., he gets ready for bed and has the lights out by 9:00 p.m.

What do you think will happen when Alex and Ben arrive for class the following day? What about the following week, month, or year? Who is better off: the student diligently doing homework or the student diligently *not* doing homework?

Of course, the above scenario is both idealized and contrived, but it's based on an inescapable fact: homework takes time. In some cases, it takes a lot of time. This means homework comes at a significant <u>opportunity cost</u>. When students are doing homework, they are necessarily *not* practising football or playing music with friends, *not* spending time with Mum and Dad, and *not* reading for pleasure.

Which begs the question: is homework worth the hundreds of millions of hours students collectively spend on it each year? And what about the millions of hours teachers collectively spend marking and assessing this work? And let's not forget the time spent on conflicts between parents and children, or the confrontations between teachers and students.

Is homework truly worth all this trouble?

DOING MY HOMEWORK

Of all the different fields that constitute educational research, you'd be hard pressed to find one more polarized than that exploring the value of homework. Even a cursory glance at the last century of literature will turn up comments ranging from calls to increase homework to pleas to abandon homework altogether.

Similarly, among academic and educational communities, you will find a wide spectrum of opinions ranging from staunch supporters to avid critics. Even across eras, the pendulum has swung from a dominant anti-homework movement in the early 1900s (California passed a law in 1901, which was revoked in 1917, that banned homework for students younger than 15 years old) to a strong Cold War influenced pro-homework movement in the late 20th century.

Among all this debate, the argument in favour of setting regular homework appears to be based upon a number of key assumptions. Let's consider each in turn.

Assumption #1: *Homework is an essential part of school.*

For many teachers, assigning homework is a lot like eating dinner at night: it's something that is part of the daily routine. In her book *Rethinking Homework*, University of Missouri professor Dr Cathy Vatterott writes:

> *Homework is a long-standing education tradition that, until recently, has seldom been questioned. The concept of homework has become so engrained in U.S. culture that the word homework is part of the common vernacular.*

So prevalent has it become that this concept has bled beyond the classroom. Many employers now set homework for new or prospective employees, coaches set homework for professional athletes, and even psychologists set homework for their patients.

This apparent compulsion to set homework is in part because of its historical association with the concept of 'rigour'. Because homework is usually graded by teachers themselves, it's easy to see how a perception might develop that rigorous teachers set more homework, while lazy teachers set less. In this sense, homework becomes a kind of 'badge of honour': good teachers must be willing to give up more of their personal time to ensure their students undertake more learning.

Contributing to this perception is the fact that most teachers and parents are the product of an education system that has long valued homework. Our teachers set homework and it worked fine for us, so why should we challenge an apparently legitimised system?

This kind of inertia is hard to shake. Despite the changing face of education, there remains a pervasive expectation among most individuals that homework is an essential habit we are expected to foster. Oddly, it can be hard to pin down the source of this expectation. In a strange kind of cyclical paradox, often teachers feel that schools expect homework, while schools feel that parents expect homework, while parents feel that teachers expect homework. In the end, it's difficult to determine who's driving this train.

In practice, these expectations likely fuel each other. But why do so many believe that we need homework in the first place? It's interesting to consider who would be the most disappointed if homework were to suddenly disappear. Would students be upset? Doubtful. Would teachers rue the lost opportunity to grade assignments? Unlikely. Would parents long for the 'good old days' when they got to nag and hassle their children to do their homework? Probably not.

But of course, we can't abolish homework, because…

<u>Assumption #2</u>: *Homework helps students develop self-regulation skills.*

It is true that you can instil an almost Pavlovian discipline in students through simple reward and punishment (an issue we'll explore further in Chapter 8). It takes only a few gold stars or detentions to encourage many students to regularly complete their homework. The logic is that this ongoing homework will lead students to develop study skills, time management skills, and independent learning skills. Presumably, these are skills that teachers don't have ample time to fully nurture in the classroom, so students must independently develop them at home.

Although this sounds plausible, there is an absolute dearth of research to support (or refute) this assumption. In fact, a recent review only returned five published articles since 1986 that explored the link between homework and student self-regulation skills. Of these, only one conducted an experimental intervention, while the remainder merely assessed correlations.

Regarding the one paper that conducted an experimental intervention, the data did show that homework could significantly improve student self-efficacy, self-reflection, and time management. But here's the twist: the homework these students were assigned explicitly explored self-efficacy, self-reflection, and time management strategies. In other words, self-regulation was not a by-product of completing the homework, it *was* the homework. Demonstrating that students can improve self-regulation skills by committing time to explicitly learning those skills is no different from demonstrating that students can learn a second language by committing time to explicitly learning that language.

The remaining four correlational papers all demonstrated that students who score higher on scales of self-regulation often complete more homework. Unfortunately, as the authors all rightly pointed out, this correlation in no way suggests a causation, and in fact can easily be understood in the opposite direction. While it's possible that students might develop self-regulation skills by completing more homework, it's equally plausible that students who already possess these skills simply have a larger capacity for homework.

In the end, none of this work speaks to the assumption that homework drives the development of discipline. As University of Arizona professor Etta Kralovec has plainly stated:

> *There's been no research done on whether homework teaches responsibility, self-discipline, or motivation. That's just a value judgment. The counterargument can just as easily be made that homework teaches kids to cheat, to do the least amount of work, or to get by.*

From a personal perspective, as I consider my 15 years of high school classroom teaching, this concept makes me feel particularly uneasy. I know that, for the most part, I set homework that I thought was meaningful. I also leveraged my relationship with students to encourage homework completion. But looking back, if I'm really being honest, I can't be sure what habits I was actually fostering in my students. Did they truly hone their study skills, or did they merely learn how to play the game of grades? Did they develop time management skills, or did they frequently complete assignments during the 5 minutes prior to class? Did they ever practise independent learning, or did they always rely on me to tell them what work was relevant?

When homework is neither particularly engaging nor inherently motivating, educators have no choice but to rely on extrinsic motivation to drive compliance. For the most part, this works – but there's no evidence to suggest that it engenders self-regulation. In fact, the only thing rewards might engender is a basic form of obedience.

But this might not be a bad thing, because…

Assumption #3: *Students must accept obedience to succeed in the 'real world'.*

It's important for students to obediently complete work they don't particularly care for because non-enjoyable work is a natural condition of the 'real world'. As adults, we all must regularly perform mundane tasks, like filing our taxes, renewing our car insurance, and sitting through professional training seminars. None of these things are deeply meaningful to most of us, and in a perfect world we wouldn't have to do them. Unfortunately, obedience dictates that we must tick these boxes to avoid punishment.

But here's the thing: while failing to file taxes carries real social consequences, failing to compete an extra hour of schoolwork while at home does not. The problem with this line of thinking becomes obvious when you recognize the clear distinction between the mundane tasks adults face (which serve as the motor of society) and those we impose onto children (which carry little to no broad social significance). Nevertheless, in the world of education, we have decided to conflate the two.

This philosophy is perhaps best captured by author Alfie Kohn, who writes that premature exposure to practices like compulsory homework 'is rationalized by invoking a notion called *BGUTI*: Better Get Used To It. The logic here is that we have to prepare [students] for the bad things that are going to be done to [them] later... by doing it to [them] now.'

BGUTI sounds a little ridiculous, both as an acronym and as a justification for homework, doesn't it? It feels like we are imagining an unnecessarily pessimistic future for our children in which 'success' is dependent upon obediently complying with the requests of superiors and completing whatever routine tasks are imposed.

The entire exercise becomes even more questionable when we consider the full cost of homework – the activities, social interactions, and other opportunities students are necessarily missing out on in order to learn the lessons of BGUTI; opportunities which may prove equally (if not more) relevant to the 'real world'.

Could it be possible that this practice is nothing more than a self-fulfilling prophecy? That rather than preparing students for modern society, BGUTI actually fashions modern society in its own image?

But hey – maybe it is all worth it because...

Assumption #4: *Homework boosts learning.*

Now we're getting to the crux of the issue. Over the last 75 years, an extensive body of research has accumulated, which – as previously noted – supports the entire spectrum of potential viewpoints on homework.

Unfortunately, almost all of this research suffers from various methodological challenges:

- Many studies are correlational, making it impossible to concretely determine the effect of homework on learning.

- Homework does not occur in a vacuum and, unfortunately, many studies fail to account for variations in classroom learning and instruction that support homework.

- Many studies rely on students' often inaccurate (if not outright fallacious) memory of how much time they spent completing homework and which learning techniques they employed.

- Many studies fail to elucidate the type, quality, or make-up of varied homework assignments.

- Many studies define and measure learning only according to grades and/or test scores.

These challenges aside, there is a wealth of data available to help us better orient our decision-making. In general, this work demonstrates that homework does have a positive effect on student learning. However, once we move beyond generalities into specifics, a much more convoluted picture emerges. Let's start by delineating between age ranges.

There is a clear consensus that homework confers little to no learning benefits among primary years students. In fact, global effect sizes range between 0.0 and 0.2, meaning the correlation between homework and learning would be classified as 'below small'.

The reasons for this are likely twofold. First, without advanced neurological maturation, few young students have developed strong inhibitory mechanisms. This makes it incredibly difficult for them to sustain attention, and leaves them highly susceptible to the myriad distractions in the home. Second, because of a lack of experience, young students often (and understandably) employ ineffective strategies that do little to advance learning. For instance, whereas older students typically devote study time to focusing on material they struggle with, younger students typically devote study time to focusing on material they already comprehend.

Fortunately, these two issues can be mitigated through adult intervention. When parents participate in a young child's homework by offering accurate and constructive feedback, they can help maintain attention and ensure the use of effective learning strategies. Unfortunately, as a result of varied social, economic, and familial circumstances, not all students have access to the type of adult support which might make homework meaningful at this young age.

When we shift our focus to older students, the news becomes slightly better. Homework appears to have a small impact on learning in middle years (global effect sizes range between 0.2 and 0.4) and a moderate impact on learning in upper years (global effect sizes range between 0.5 and 0.7). Although the reasons for these gains are still up for debate, likely explanations include the increased development of cognitive control, a more consistent implementation of effective learning strategies, and an increased motivation to succeed.

Perhaps the most important research finding with regard to homework is that any measurable correlation between duration and outcome is *not* linear. Put simply, more homework does not necessarily mean more learning. Rather, homework can generally benefit learning only up to a certain time point; beyond this point, homework can often *impair* learning. Among primary year students, this point appears to be ~15 minutes; among middle year students it appears to be ~45 minutes; and among upper year students it appears to be ~60 minutes.

This means homework can indeed improve learning, but only when it's done in shorter stints than most people would assume.

Unfortunately, most schools greatly exceed these learning limits. Although it's difficult to arrive at a precise figure, in the US, the UK, and Australia, primary year students are assigned an average of 35 minutes of homework per night, while middle and upper year students are assigned an average of 90 minutes per night.

Do you see the problem? Herein lies the primary issue of opportunity cost. Many schools assign too much homework, which needlessly pushes students beyond their natural 'limits'. Beyond potentially harming learning, this practice also reduces the time students have to undertake personally meaningful activities which may drive different forms of social, emotional, and personal learning not typically reflected in exams.

Beyond learning, there is research linking increased homework to decreased wellbeing. Some surveys report that approximately 60% of students cite homework as a primary source of stress (compared to less than 1% who describe it as a non-stressor), while upwards of 30% of students in some countries are categorized as 'clinically depressed' as a result of pressures from unceasing academic work.

This is a crucial aspect of the opportunity cost argument that is too often overlooked. It has long been known that pursuing personal passions with like-minded peers is a great way to combat stress and support wellbeing. By reducing the amount of personal time students have at home, there is a high likelihood that homework is significantly contributing to the sharp rise in student stress and mental illness reported around the world.

SO NOW THEN...

What can we conclude from this long, ambiguous story of homework?

First, homework generally appears to be a powerful tool that can support student learning in certain circumstances. Unfortunately, this power is often used with little regard for the opportunity cost involved. Perhaps an ideal approach would be to neither exalt nor vilify homework, but simply to understand its benefits and boundaries, and employ the tool accordingly.

Second, it's always important to strategically consider the format that homework assumes. At a practical level, several analyses have demonstrated that homework largely boosts learning when it is task-based and focused on the practice/rehearsal of previously learned knowledge or skills. Whenever homework introduces novel material, requires deep consideration, or takes a project-based approach, learning diminishes significantly. This is likely due to the necessity of expert guidance and feedback when undertaking deeper forms of learning – a scaffold that is mostly unavailable (at least in real time) when working from home. As such, structuring homework around material which students are at least moderately acquainted with will generally produce the best outcomes.

But beyond mere practical considerations, would it be possible to reimagine the format of homework in a way that cultivates a love of learning (rather than simple obedience), or inspires collaboration between children and their parents (rather than isolated work)? There are certainly many different forms this could take, but opportunity cost could be greatly diminished if homework were used to embrace activities students would normally undertake and were used to increase motivation by fostering relationships.

Third, long-form homework should be dropped from all primary schools: there is no compelling or even reasonable argument to be made for its inclusion. With that said, there is strong evidence to suggest that reading with parents is a great way for young learners to develop their cognitive and emotional capacity while simultaneously boosting their reading skills. Perhaps this idea aligns with the broader ambition of homework alluded to in the previous paragraph.

With regard to secondary schools, short-form homework should remain the default. Additional work should only be assigned when it conveys a clear, demonstrable learning purpose (and never as a pretext to signal teaching 'rigour'). Furthermore, it might make sense to include students in the homework setting process. Seeing as it's their time, their effort, and their learning on the line, perhaps it's worthwhile getting their input.

Fourth, remember that homework occurs at *home*. Homework should not be about schools reaching into the homes of students in order to extend lesson time. As Maya Angelou, the great American poet wrote, 'The ache for home lives in all of us. The safe place where we can go as we are and not be questioned.' Any homework assigned should not simply extend lessons because of inadequate time or organization during the school day.

In the end, we return to where we began: opportunity cost. If homework is to be employed, then it's important that the associated benefits outweigh those that might be gleaned from other activities students will necessarily be sacrificing. Unfortunately, when research suggests that students undertake too much homework, and as a result experience reduced wellbeing, we have an obligation to scrutinize this endeavour. Is it possible to assign less but better homework that boosts learning while freeing up more time for children to engage in sports, play in bands, talk to parents, and read for pleasure at home? Surely the non-academic benefits of such activities must outweigh the opportunity cost associated with pushing homework beyond the limits of student learning.

CHAPTER 5

MINDSET – THE PROBLEM WITH HYPE

"IF WE HAVE THE TRUTH, IT CANNOT BE HARMED BY INVESTIGATION. IF WE HAVE NOT THE TRUTH, IT OUGHT TO BE HARMED."

– J. REUBEN CLARK

You're probably familiar with the story of Roger Bannister, the famous British athlete who in 1954 became the first person in recorded history to run a mile in under 4 minutes. His official time of 3:59 managed to just barely shave the perceived biomechanical limitations of human running.

At the same time, it obliterated a hidden psychological barrier.

Only six weeks after Bannister defied the odds, Australian runner John Landy would better his record by 1 second. Over the next few decades, nearly 1500 runners (including a handful of high school students) would break the 4-minute mile and achieve a feat long thought to be impossible.

Everything had changed. Yet almost nothing had changed.

Humans did not suddenly become faster or more efficient in their oxygen consumption. It's true that athletic technology was evolving, but in a sport as pure as middle distance running, there were no carbon fibre wings or sharkskin swimsuits to significantly increase speed.

No. The impact of Bannister's 3:59 mile was more profound. As Yoram Wind and Colin Crook observe in their book *The Power of Impossible Thinking*:

> *What changed was the mental model. The runners of the past had been held back by a mindset that said they could not surpass the four-minute mile. When that limit was broken, the others saw that they could do something they had previously thought impossible.*

The story of Roger Bannister is a story about mindset. It's a story about the impact that our internal beliefs can have on ability and performance. It has become legend – and legends inspire us. They become parables imbued with simple yet profound lessons that we can all apply to our daily lives and personal practices.

Sometimes, however, this can be a problem.

THE FUZZY FANTASY

In 2006, Stanford University Professor Carol Dweck published one of the most popular and impactful books to have emerged from modern psychology. The 277 pages of *Mindset* have been printed over 2 million times and translated into more than 20 languages.

With Bannister's 3:59 mile in mind, consider the Google Books description of Dweck's book:

> *Carol S. Dweck, Ph.D., discovered a simple but ground-breaking idea: the power of mindset. In this brilliant book, she shows how success in school, work, sports, the arts, and almost every area of human endeavour can be dramatically influenced by how we think about our talents and abilities.*

Sound familiar?

Dweck certainly didn't invent the concept of beliefs affecting performance. But she did write a brilliant book that captures the spirit of this idea. The research is compelling and the included anecdotes about Michael Jordan, Charles Darwin, and Cindy Sherman are powerful. In addition, the core concept is charmingly simple for teachers: If we can get students to *believe* that they can improve at science, maths, or music through practice, then they *will* improve.

For those unfamiliar with Dweck's mindset philosophy, you may want to watch her 2014 TEDx Talk, during which she outlines the essence of her thesis:

- Human beings can be divided into two distinct mindset categories.

- Those with a *fixed mindset* believe that abilities (including things like intelligence, music, athleticism, etc.) are fundamentally unchangeable. People are born with innate talents, and there's little we can do to change them.

- Those with a *growth mindset* believe that abilities are fundamentally malleable. People are born with no pre-set limitations, and all talents can be developed through explicit practice and effort.

Mindset is a system that helps us make sense of the world. Was I born to be good at tennis (i.e. my abilities were genetically predetermined)? Or was I born to be neutral at tennis (i.e. my abilities were developed through practice)?

The true sticking power of this theory derives from what researchers call <u>face validity</u>. Mindset 'feels' right and appears effective because, experientially, it generally is. People with a fixed mindset frequently don't bother with practice and, accordingly, rarely show improvement. 'I was bad at tennis as a child, so there was no point in my practising. I'm still bad at tennis as an adult. See, abilities don't change!' Conversely, people with a growth mindset are motivated to practise and, accordingly, frequently improve. 'I was bad at tennis as a child, so I practised a lot. Today I'm really good at tennis. See, abilities do change!'

Mindset, whether fixed or growth, is the perfect example of a self-fulfilling prophecy.

The other really attractive element of mindset theory is that it suggests things like motivation, growth and ability are largely contingent on personal belief. Your mindset is a thought; and, like all thoughts, it can be changed.

Many teachers have stories of those unfortunate parent–teacher conferences where Mum or Dad, sitting next to their child, says something like: 'I'm not surprised to hear that he's struggling in maths. I've never been any good at maths myself. The poor kid got my genes!' Luckily, mindset-informed teachers know that there is hope! Even when Mum or Dad are nurturing unhelpful beliefs in their child, such teachers can play a significant role in influencing motivation by helping him change his thinking.

Clearly, then, it's important that educators work hard to foster a growth mindset amongst students. In fact, maybe it's imperative – at least, this is what Carol Dweck's data would suggest. Dweck's early research has demonstrated that a growth mindset can elevate cognitive performance, increase achievement, boost grades, and even help students persist in the face of challenging problems.

And so, for caring teachers who want their students to learn and grow, it appears Dweck has discovered the magic bullet. Foster a growth mindset, and students will work hard and learn well.

But, here's the problem: although mindset might be powerful in controlled laboratories, it doesn't work nearly as well in actual classrooms.

THE HARD REALITY

In 2018, researchers from Case Western Reserve University published the most comprehensive meta-analysis of mindset ever compiled. These researchers examined 273 studies investigating the link between mindset and academic achievement as well as 43 studies investigating the impact of mindset interventions on academic achievement. Altogether, the data from over 400,000 students revealed that the 'correlation between mindset and academic achievement is very weak', and that there is only 'a very small overall effect of mindset interventions on academic achievement'.

For most students in most situations, mindset seems to have little to no impact on achievement.

But, wait – what about Dweck's original research? In 2019, Yue Li and Timothy Bates from the University of Edinburgh conducted a replication of her work. After compiling their data, these researchers concluded that:

> *Mindsets about the nature of intelligence have near-zero effects on grades and no effect on general cognitive ability. In the specific case of responses to failure, neither children's internalized mindset nor their activated beliefs about whether intelligence is or is not fixed had an impact on performance.*

We could simply leave it here: new research is overwhelmingly proving that mindset isn't the panacea many people were led to believe it was. However, there is more to learn. What larger lessons can we glean from the meteoric rise of mindset within education?

Four in particular come to mind.

IT'S ALL IN THE ABSTRACT

The first thing mindset teaches us is that almost nobody reads the research.

By some estimates, 2 million peer-reviewed articles are published annually. Unfortunately, statistics show that up to 40% of articles within the social sciences and up to 80% of papers within the humanities (of which education is a part) will never be cited. In fact, some estimates suggest that research articles are read in their entirety by only 10 people.

To see this in action, try a simple experiment. Find a typical classroom teacher (there are 90 million in the world to choose from) and ask how many peer-reviewed journal articles s/he has read in the last 6 months. Spoiler alert – the answer will be zero. If it's not, then you didn't find a 'typical' classroom teacher. It's not that educational research is unreadable, inaccessible, or unrelatable; it's that, professionally speaking, teachers are all-consumed by their teaching! Most simply do not have the time or incentive to play detective and trawl through the millions of published academic studies just to find the bits relevant to their practice.

If you're a dedicated educator, you can almost certainly empathize with this catch-22. Teachers are so immersed in trying to deliver the highest quality evidence-informed instruction that they don't have time to read the evidence itself.

So, where do many of us gather our evidence-informed ideas if not from the evidence itself? We get them in digest form from conferences, workshops, books, webinars, and TED talks. Importantly, after attempting to implement these stripped-down extrapolations in our classrooms, we are too often left wondering, *why didn't that work for me?* Over time, most teachers will come to discover that many of the popularized practices we are encouraged to apply in actual classrooms are near-fictionalized interpretations of tenuous theories developed in heavily-controlled laboratories (once again, we are confronted with the issue of 'translation' as explored in Chapter 2).

At this point, it would be all too easy for academics to cry foul and complain that their work has simply been misinterpreted. However, although this objection would certainly be valid in some cases, misinterpretation first requires an accurate and realistic representation of research by the academics themselves.

Let's consider the case of mindset specifically. Across a variety of popular publications, Carol Dweck has offered the following statements:

- '[Mindset] has profound effects on student... learning and school achievement.'

- '[Mindset] can matter even more than cognitive factors for students' academic performance.'

- '[M]indsets play a key role in math and science achievement.'

- '[I]f we changed student mindsets we could boost their achievement.'

- '[E]mphasis on growth not only increases intellectual achievement but can also advance conflict resolution... in the Middle East [e.g. between Israelis and Palestinians].'

It becomes difficult to maintain this theory has been 'misinterpreted' when the developer herself has made exaggerated, inaccurate, and (in some cases) erroneous claims that mindset can boost academic achievement, that it is more important than cognitive factors for learning, and that it can presumably foster world peace.

In the end, I don't imagine teachers will suddenly find the time to meaningfully engage with the ever-expanding body of academic research. As such, it's imperative that researchers honestly and accurately represent their work. Furthermore, it's worth reiterating the ideas put forth in Chapters 1 and 2 that theory is different than practice, and that emergent properties will likely skew any laboratory-based data. Regardless of the specific conclusions drawn by academics, teachers will always need to prescriptively translate work to their own unique contexts in order to derive utility.

THE DEVIL IS IN THE DETAILS

The second thing mindset teaches us is that details matter.

Mindset theory captured attention because of its simplicity and elegance. It not only helped to explain student behaviour, but also provided an intuitive pivot from the praise-based approach of the 1990s.

The evidence that drove this theory, unfortunately, is very limited in its educational generalizability. For instance, in her seminal 1998 research, Dweck demonstrated that students were more likely to engage with challenging content when they were praised for their *effort* as opposed to their *intelligence*. Unfortunately, this impact was only measured immediately after students received praise – as opposed to minutes, hours, or days later. This suggests that what Dweck uncovered was likely the well-documented short-term impact of expectancy priming (whereby students will quickly adapt their behaviour based upon what a teacher signals as being 'important') rather than any long-term impact of mindset.

This, in part, helps explain why the 2019 replication study cited earlier found 'no support for the idea that fixed [mindsets] are harmful, or that [growth mindsets] play any significant role in development of cognitive ability, response to challenge, or educational attainment'. Priming is a notoriously fickle cognitive occurrence, and it's highly likely that the students used in the replication simply didn't respond to this obvious procedure. In response, Dweck has argued that the contradictory findings were due to methodological errors in the study.

Similarly, in her famous 2007 research, Dweck demonstrated a correlation between student mindset and performance on standardized maths exams. Unfortunately, the operative word here is *correlation*, as mindset was only ever measured after exams were taken. Considering the large body of research demonstrating that success breeds confidence, there's every chance this data reflects performance-driving mindset – not the other way around.

To address this issue of correlation, Dweck and her colleagues attempted an explicit 8-week mindset intervention meant to establish direct causation. Unfortunately, this intervention was shown to have no significant impact on later maths exam performance – a finding the authors attributed to a small sample size.

Whenever 'positive' studies are accepted without scrutiny while associated 'negative' studies are dismissed on the grounds of methodology or sample size, this is a good indication that what we're dealing with is a flimsy theoretical construct of limited import and even more limited generalizability.

In the case of mindset, it becomes even more difficult to maintain the 'poor methodology' argument when one factors the meta-analysis noted earlier that found little to no correlation between mindset and academic achievement, and little to no impact of mindset interventions. Unless all 316 of the included studies contained similar methodological errors, it seems far more likely that mindset does not play the role in achievement that early interpretations of Dweck's research led many to believe.

Undeterred, in 2019, Dweck and colleagues published another study exploring the impact of an explicit mindset intervention on over 12,000 Year 9 students from 76 schools around the US. Unsurprisingly, the results demonstrated no effect overall – however, among lower achieving students (defined as students in the bottom 50% of class ranking according to final grades), the intervention was shown to increase grade point average by approximately 0.1 out of 4.0 points over the course of 1 school year. Needless to say, this finding was met with excitement.

Here's the problem: in medicine, researchers must differentiate between statistical significance and clinical significance. Statistical significance occurs when any treatment effect is shown to not have occurred by chance. Clinical significance, on the other hand, occurs when any treatment is shown to confer greater impact than current practices. Importantly, these two forms of significance are dissociable. Imagine that I run an experiment testing a new diet pill. Now imagine that, after six months of taking my pill, everyone in my experiment loses one pound. Seeing as every participant lost the same amount of weight, my treatment effect would be statistically significant (not having occurred by chance). However, seeing as the weight lost was only 1 pound over 6 months, my treatment effect would be clinically irrelevant (as there are dozens of other treatments that can confer a much larger impact in much less time).

Demonstrating that a mindset intervention can improve the grade point average of a subset of students by 0.1 out of 4.0 points over one school year might be statistically significant, but it is clinically irrelevant. There are dozens of highly effective interventions (including tutoring, study groups, explicitly teaching time management skills, etc.) that confer far more benefit for far more students over the course of a year. Furthermore, with an impact of 0.1 grade points per year, this intervention would see only ~5% of struggling students shift their final grade. Assuming there were 1.5 million Year 9 students on track to fail this year, this intervention ensures 1.425 million would still fail – statistically significant, but clinically irrelevant.

With that said, there's an important caveat. Mindset interventions have been shown to demonstrate an impact among economically disadvantaged students at risk of dropping out of school (although the specifics and reliability of this impact remain unclear). Their experience within an environment that fosters educational apathy has logically conditioned them to view academic study as a waste of time. Accordingly, if mindset interventions can help to keep at-risk students in school at a clinically significant level, then it might be a godsend for this particular student population.

Nevertheless, if we recognize that mindset interventions are not a universal cure-all and appear to only impact a specific group of students in an unreliable manner, is it worth employing them on a school-wide basis?

Considering the evidence outlined above, the answer is likely no.

SUBTLETY FIRST

The third thing mindset teaches us is that teaching is an incredibly subtle craft.

Recently, I asked John Hendry, recipient of an Order of Australia Medal for his lifetime contribution to education, what rituals he engaged in when preparing for his lessons. This was his response:

> *Let me tell you about the seven steps I always took: they were the last seven steps before I got to any classroom door – when I would gather myself and acknowledge how grateful I was for the privilege of helping guide the lives of my students. You never know exactly what lies behind that door – other than the guarantee that it will be different from anything you've experienced before and that it will be wonderful.*

This beautifully illustrates the point of divergence between the laboratory and the classroom. While great research attempts to isolate and eliminate variables, great teaching attempts to embrace and amplify variables. Each school, each cohort, each lesson, and each student is unique and wonderful. And so, teachers thrive in the liminal space between chameleon-like adaptability and cement-like integrity.

This form of professional malleability is achieved through the subtle, fluid, and often subconscious harnessing of the 'tools of the trade'– which are countless. One recent analysis from Brown University reviewed the impact of 481 educational tools across 242 randomized controlled trials and found that the majority (including mindset) had a very small impact on student achievement. Most tools simply do not, in and of themselves, produce large gains.

The reason for this is *the teacher*. Teachers (and the craft of teaching) are the primary mediating factor that determines whether or not a tool will impact learning. Mindset, motivation, hope, joy, inspiration, resilience, and grit have every chance to boost student learning – but only if they are meaningfully and practically filtered through the teacher.

When we multiply the infinitely variable social learning environment by the infinitely complex mediating factor of the teacher, it becomes easy to appreciate how each class, each tool, and each intervention will be 'different to anything experienced before'.

Many, including Dweck, appear to have been caught out by this fact. As she explained in a recent interview: 'In the beginning... we did not recognise the complexity of the implementation.' Mindset does not possess any magical properties. Rather, like all tools, it is but a small component of the real magic produced by effective teachers every day.

TO FAIL IS TO LEARN... SOMETIMES

The fourth thing mindset teaches us is that many of us are confused about 'failure'.

For those with a growth mindset, failure is a natural and necessary step towards betterment. We can only learn to walk by falling countless times. Conversely, for those with a fixed mindset, failure is further evidence that humans possess innate limitations. Amongst these individuals, failure is seen as a direct reflection of identity; accordingly, it makes perfect sense to avoid failure at all costs by sidestepping challenges.

Here is where things get messy.

There's a famous quote from basketball legend Michael Jordan that reads:

I've missed more than 9000 shots in my career. I've lost almost 300 games. Twenty-six times, I've been trusted to take the game winning shot and missed. I've failed over and over and over again in my life. And that is why I succeed.

Let's assume that this was actually said by Jordan (and not created by a copywriter working in Nike's marketing department). It certainly is inspirational and uplifting. But let's break it down:

- 'I've missed more than 9000 shots in my career' – *true.*

- 'I've lost almost 300 games' – *true.*

- 'Twenty-six times, I've been trusted to take the game winning shot and missed' – *true.*

- 'I've failed over and over and over again in my life. And that is why I succeed' – *false*.

Jordan didn't succeed because he failed – he succeeded because he practised. And practised. And practised. He succeeded because he was more dedicated, more disciplined, and more determined than his peers. In fact, Tim Grover, Jordan's physical trainer, described him as 'the most competitive individual I'd ever met'.

To be fair, Jordan certainly had a growth mindset and was willing to fail in order to push himself to greater heights. But here's the key distinction: 99% of his failures happened during practice.

When Jordan failed during games, he simply failed. It was demoralizing. It felt awful. He wished it didn't happen. In Game 1 of the 1991 NBA Finals, with 7 seconds on the clock, Jordan had a chance to win the game with a routine (by his standards) jump shot. He missed. He failed. His team lost. In Game 2 of the 1992 Finals, it happened again. In Game 4 of the 1997 Finals, and Game 5 of the 1998 Finals, same story. Time and again, Jordan failed on the biggest stage, and each time he suffered significantly from it.

But here is where we start to recognize the important difference between learning states and performance states.

When mistakes and failure occur in a performance state, it's difficult to construe them as positive. Sure, when Jordan failed on the basketball court, it was a relatively trivial matter (even though teams never get a chance to replay lost games). But, for cardiac surgeons performing open-heart surgery, or police officers pursuing high-speed vehicles, or air traffic controllers juggling dozens of outgoing flights, failure can often be fatal.

However, failure is crucial and absolutely necessary in a learning state. Amongst those with a growth mindset, this is when failure is truly embraced. If I'm ever forced to undergo heart surgery, I hope that my surgeon failed often while learning at university, and made many mistakes while refining her skills during training.

Let's shift our focus back to school – perhaps to a typical Year 10 maths class. How clear is the meaning of failure in this context? Is it good to put my hand up and get the answer wrong? Is it good that I failed to get half of my homework practice equations correct? And what about getting 40% of my end-of-week quiz questions wrong – is that positive or negative failure?

In other words, is school primarily a *learning* institution or a *performance* institution? What does it reward? What does it celebrate? For what are the accolades given and trophies awarded? Who gets to walk across the stage and shake the principal's hand at the end of the year?

There's the mess.

A growth mindset requires one to fully embrace failure. Unfortunately, failure only helps students succeed during learning – which means that failure and mindset can only be meaningfully embraced when schools are understood as learning institutions. Unfortunately, when the focus of schools is predominately on performance, failure becomes decidedly negative and mindset becomes largely irrelevant.

SO NOW THEN...

Mindset in education is a wonderful example of hype overshadowing reality. In this instance, the loudest voice telling the most compelling story successfully convinced many that education could be elevated simply by changing student beliefs without changing the context in which those same students work. This is analogous to fad diets promising you can lose weight without changing your eating patterns or exercise regime.

Though mindset is undoubtedly a powerful force, academics must represent it more accurately and educators must consider it in a more nuanced manner. If we are going to commit academic resources to this theory, what benefits can we meaningfully expect? Furthermore, what larger, structural changes must be implemented at the school-wide level in order to realize these benefits?

Seeing as mindset cannot substitute for effective learning strategies, there's a good chance it will never be shown to reliably boost traditional academic outcomes among most students. Perhaps, though, that's not what mindset is meant to do. Perhaps it's meant merely to inspire students to think differently and ask better questions. To be fair, this would be a wonderful outcome – however, it's important we first specify these possible outcomes, and then devise a means to determine if mindset truly influences each.

Until the impact of mindset can be clearly determined and reliably demonstrated, it will remain little more than an educational fad leading to significant disenchantment in the long run.

CHAPTER 6

21ST CENTURY SKILLS – THE PROBLEM WITH TRANSFER

"THE ILLITERATE OF THE 21ST CENTURY WILL NOT BE THOSE WHO CANNOT READ AND WRITE, BUT THOSE WHO CANNOT LEARN, UNLEARN, AND RELEARN."

– ALVIN TOFFLER

There is a popular argument that has been circulating around education for quite some time – see if you recognize it:

> *School is a remnant of the Industrial Revolution. We teach kids from standardized curricula while they sit quietly in rows simply repeating what they've been told. Though this may have worked well to churn out efficient factory workers, times have changed. Today, schools have to do more than build employees; they must forge holistic, confident citizens of the 21st century. To this end, it's time to ditch outdated methods and embrace those four competencies (termed C21 skills) most relevant to our modern world: creativity, critical thinking, collaboration, and communication.*

There are two reasons why this argument is unintentionally bizarre. First, it reflects a profound misunderstanding of the history of schooling. Standardized curricula were first proposed in 1576 by Parisian educator Petrus Ramus in response to the explosion of available information generated by the printing press. By the mid 17th century, curricula were widely used throughout Europe – over 100 years before the start of the Industrial Revolution. Furthermore, if you look at artwork depicting medieval schooling or renaissance scholasticism, you will see students sitting in rows, scribing notes while listening to an instructor. This organization doesn't reflect an industrial model; it reflects a millennia-old method of teaching.

Second, for all the adoration heaped upon the four C21 skills, very few people have stopped to ask where they came from. Without question, creativity, critical thinking, collaboration, and communication are important – but who elevated these particular skills above the countless other meaningful proficiencies? What about health, integrity, morality, kindness, dedication, trustworthiness, loyalty, or perseverance?

It turns out, the C21 skills were established at a breakfast meeting held at the Adams Mark Hotel in Dallas, Texas, on 15 November 2002. This breakfast was sponsored by the National Education Association, endorsed by the U.S. Department of Education, and involved 6 parties: AOL/Time Warner, Apple, Cisco, Dell, Microsoft, and SAP. Following this meeting, these companies released a document outlining the aforementioned four 21st century learning skills, the very first sentence of which reads:

Successful businesses are looking for employees who can adapt to changing needs, juggle multiple responsibilities and routinely make decisions on their own... there [is] an evolving demand for 21st Century Skills in our economy.

That's right – the C21 skills progressive educators use to rebel against a model of schooling meant only to churn out efficient employees were hand-picked by businesses as those skills which schools must focus on in order to churn out efficient employees.

While I firmly believe school is meant for more than employment, that is not the point I wish to make here (rest assured, we'll tackle this issue in Chapter 10). Rather, I've told this story to highlight something seemingly obvious: many universities require students to successfully demonstrate mastery of the four C21 skills as a condition for earning a degree. Seeing as these skills were explicitly selected by employers, it follows that new graduates should be workplace ready.

Here's the rub: this process isn't working. An estimated 50% of entry-level hires don't reach the 18-month mark of employment, while the remaining 50% require up to 24 months before they consistently demonstrate those C21 skills they purportedly mastered while at university. In fact, so frustrated have businesses become with entry-level college graduates, that many of the world's most prominent companies (including Apple and Google) no longer require employees to hold a four-year degree and, instead, rely on in-house strategies to evaluate and ultimately develop C21 skills.

Importantly, this phenomenon is not confined to first-time employees. An estimated 50% of new hires across *every* level of employment – from entry to executive – fail within 18 months. In one high-profile example, the struggling American retailer JCPenney chose Ron Johnson as CEO in 2011 based largely on the deep creativity he demonstrated while conceiving the ultra-successful Apple Store. Unfortunately, 17 months and 5 billion dollars of lost revenue later, Johnson was fired without ever demonstrating his patented creative flair.

Similarly, when tech giant Hewlett-Packard hired Carly Fiorina as CEO in 1999, it was based largely on the impressive team building and collaboration prowess she demonstrated at Lucent Technologies. Unfortunately, after a highly contentious merger and the subsequent layoff of over 30,000 employees, most pundits agree that these collaborative skills never made the jump between businesses.

The fact that all people across all levels of employment struggle to move their well-established C21 skills between jobs means something deeper must be driving this pattern; something more fundamental. So, what's going on?

THE TRANSFER DILEMMA

Within education, 'transfer' refers to the ability to apply skills learned within one domain to a novel and often completely different domain. A strong argument can be made that this is the ultimate goal of schooling: although it's nice to see a student perform well on assignments and exams, most educators are more interested in developing students who can apply skills within broader domains beyond the classroom.

Most people mistakenly assume that once a skill has been mastered in one realm, it becomes freely transferable across all realms. Unfortunately, that is simply not the case. This is why many students who can perform arithmetic using digits get flustered when presented with word problems, and why many students who can evaluate historical essays stumble when presented with science essays. Beyond the classroom, this is why many people rant at their smartphones after downloading a system update (*Why can't I access my apps?*) and why they butcher meals when cooking in a friend's kitchen (*Your oven must have a different temperature than mine*).

It's an unfortunate quirk of human cognition that transfer does not happen automatically. Read that again, because it's incredibly important: *transfer does not happen automatically*. This means, regardless of how effectively a student demonstrates the four C21 skills of creativity, critical thinking, collaboration, and communication within school, these skills almost always deteriorate (for a time, at least) once outside school.

Fortunately, although transfer may not be automatic, it is not impossible – it simply requires navigating a predictable three-step process:

Step #1: Knowledge

Step #2: Contextualization

Step #3: Adaptation

Let's take a look at each of these steps in turn.

STEP #1 – KNOWLEDGE

In order to transfer any skill to a new domain, it is first required that individuals possess a deep understanding of the facts and concepts relevant to that domain. To clarify, let's do a quick experiment.

Chances are, within your particular specialty, you demonstrate strong critical thinking abilities. If you're a science teacher, you can deconstruct and challenge fringe hypotheses. If you're a principal, you can clarify and integrate multiple pedagogical frameworks. If you're a school counsellor, you can differentiate and assess subjective symptoms versus objective signs.

Recognizing that you already possess the C21 skill of critical thinking (and likely apply it every day), try resolving the following problem:

Recently, magnetoencephalographic data was published suggesting the human brain generates a very low-frequency wave (approximately 6 cycles per hour) that cannot be source localized and appears equally diffuse across all brain regions simultaneously.

Thinking critically, determine what methodological error likely led to this result – or, if this data is accurate, what does this suggest about ephaptic coupling within the brain?

Unless you're a neuroscientist or an engineer, you likely weren't able to make heads or tails of this scenario. It turns out, all the critical thinking skills in the world become obsolete when you try to apply them to information you can't comprehend.

Put simply, <u>knowledge precedes skills</u>.

To see this principle in action, consider the following study. Students classified as possessing either 'strong' or 'weak' reading comprehension skills were asked to read a passage about the sport of baseball. Importantly, some students already knew much about this sport (watched it on TV, played on a team, collected playing cards, etc.), whilst others knew very little. When quizzed about what they understood from the reading, here's what happened:

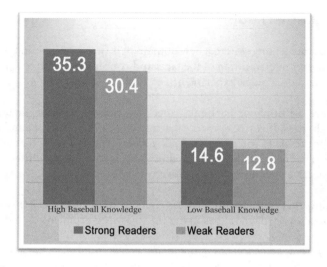

Clearly, the skill of reading comprehension had a limited bearing on performance. Rather, possessing prior knowledge of baseball facts determined whether or not students were able to understand the text. As noted by the researchers, 'students with high reading ability but low knowledge of baseball were no more capable of recall or summarization than were students with low reading ability and low knowledge of baseball.'

This explains why Ron Johnson failed to carry over his creativity from Apple to JCPenney. It's roundly accepted that he started making changes without ever taking the time to first learn about the store, its history, or the shopping preferences of its customers.

Before moving on, it's worth asking: what about Google? Sure, you may not know what magnetoencephalography or ephaptic coupling are, but you could easily access this information on the internet.

Unfortunately, application of the four C21 skills requires a significant investment of time. Despite what many successful individuals might report, teams aren't built in a minute, tools aren't created in an hour, and answers aren't established in a day. It's only after domain knowledge has been *internally* embedded within long-term memory that humans can effectively apply deep cognitive skills to that knowledge. As psychologist Paul A. Kirschner notes: 'Long-term memory is now viewed as the central, dominant structure of human cognition.'

Unfortunately, when individuals know that many facts are easily accessible via *external* means (such as the internet), they commit significantly fewer facts to memory. This explains why we so often fail to remember phone numbers, e-mail addresses, or meeting schedules – because technology has allowed us to off-load memory storage onto external devices. Accordingly, even if you were to use Google to look up the definitions of magnetoencephalography and ephaptic coupling, you'd likely forget this information in rapid fashion (though you'd remember where to access it online), and be no closer to applying your C21 skills to address the question of what went wrong with the aforementioned research.

As psychologist Daniel Willingham succinctly puts it: 'The processes we most hope to engender in our students – thinking critically and logically – are not possible without background knowledge.'

STEP #2 – CONTEXTUALIZATION

After internalizing relevant knowledge, the next step on the path to effective skill transfer is using this knowledge to recharacterize skills according to the unique demands of the new domain.

It would be wonderful if skills were identical across every situation. Unfortunately, it is plainly evident that the same skill can differ significantly when applied to different contexts. For example, consider collaboration:

- In the context of performing surgery, collaboration requires individuals to *apply* their respective expertise in order to achieve a specific outcome. This often requires assertive communication with little regard for open debate.

- In the context of academic research, collaboration requires individuals to *question* their respective expertise in order to assess a hypothesized outcome. This often requires open debate with little regard for compromise.

- In the context of product design, collaboration requires individuals to develop a *shared* expertise with no clearly defined outcome. This often requires compromise with little regard for assertive communication.

The fact that definitions vary across contexts means there can be no 'all-purpose' skill directly applicable to any and every field. Rather, skills must be redefined according to the specific characteristics of each domain.

Put simply, <u>skills must be contextualized</u>.

Without contextualization, no (or incorrect) skills will emerge. This is why Carly Fiorina was unable to transfer her deep collaborative skills across companies: although she took the time to establish deep knowledge of Hewlett-Packard and its market, she never used this knowledge to recharacterize what effective collaboration would entail. Instead, she simply tried to apply the same strategies that proved successful in her previous position.

STEP #3 – ADAPTATION

After internalizing relevant knowledge and redefining skills, the final step required for effective skill transfer is consciously tweaking each skill to match its new definition. Unfortunately, this adjustment process is much easier said than done.

The reason why skill adaptation is so tricky concerns competing neural systems. It turns out that the human brain possesses a unique dual system learning apparatus that swings between active engagement and passive automaticity.

Whenever we first learn a new skill, we must consciously and effortfully engage with it. Within the brain, this active engagement is typically characterized by enhanced activity across frontal regions (thought to reflect deployment of attention and processing of new information) coupled with rhythmic activity across deeper memory networks. However, the more we practise a particular skill, the more we can begin to subconsciously and effortlessly perform it. Within the brain, this switch to passive automaticity is typically characterized by enhanced activity within the basal ganglia: a deep region heavily involved in the formation of habits and routines.

To see this switch in action, think back to when you first learned how to drive a car. Chances are you had to focus intently on the gear stick, the pedals, the steering wheel, the mirrors, the road: it was likely an overwhelming and exhausting experience. Now, think back to your last commute. Chances are you remember almost nothing about it. This is because, having mastered the art of driving, your basal ganglia can run this skill on autopilot with little to no conscious input from you.

Here's the important bit: once a skill becomes automated within a particular context, it becomes incredibly difficult to consciously access and adjust that skill outside of that context. For instance, I learned how to drive in the US, where the gear stick sits on the right. A decade ago, I moved to Australia where the gear stick sits on the left. This should have been an incredibly simple skill adjustment – but if you've ever driven a car in a foreign country, you already know how difficult it proved to be.

Put simply, <u>automaticity hinders adaptation</u>.

A set of seminal psychological experiments from the 1980s brilliantly demonstrates this principle. In this study, researchers wanted to see if a pair of students could develop savant-like memorization skills. To that end, each student spent hundreds of hours listening to, memorizing, and repeating back random strings of digits. Here's what happened:

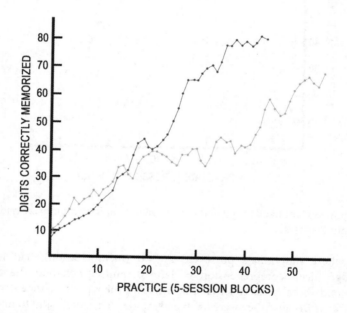

At the beginning, each student was only able to memorize and repeat back about 7 digits. However, after 50 weeks of practice, both were able to easily take in and verbally recite over 70 digits! From this we learn a very important fact: with deliberate effort and practice, any human being can come to master any skill (within physical and/or cognitive constraints, of course).

Importantly, after developing savant-like memorization skills, each student was asked to try something new. As before, they would have to listen to, memorize, and repeat back a string of information – except this time, instead of using random *digits*, the researchers would use random *letters*. With their new, powerful memorization skills in tow, this simple switch to the alphabet should have been no problem at all, right? Take a look:

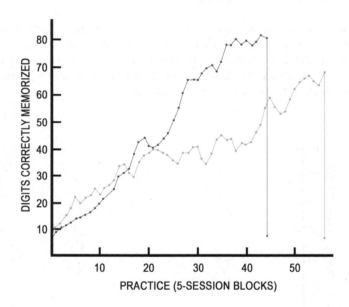

Both dropped right back to normal, and were only able to memorize and repeat back about 7 letters.

Clearly, these individuals possessed a skill (memorization), had relevant knowledge (deep comprehension of letters), and understood the context (take in and verbally recite letters). So why did their performance decline so dramatically? Because they were unable to rapidly adapt their skill to match the demands of the new domain.

Before moving on, it's worth noting that although adaption is *difficult*, it is by no means *impossible*: it simply requires conscious effort and practice. In addition, the process of skill adaptation typically moves much faster than initial skill learning. For instance, whereas it took me about six months to first learn how to drive a stick shift in the US, it only took me 1 month to adapt this skill and drive a stick shift in Australia.

Finally, it's important to recognize that even after skills have been effectively adapted, prior automated patterns have an annoying tendency to reconstitute. For instance, I have been driving in Australia from the right side of the car for over a decade. Despite this, whenever I am under stress, I often find myself getting into the left side of the car and reaching for a steering wheel that's not there: a phantom from my prior automated US driving skill.

THE ONLY FUTURE-PROOF SKILL

In summary, the process of skill transfer includes three steps: knowledge, contextualization, and adaptation. We must first internalize relevant knowledge, then synthesize these facts to establish appropriate skill definitions, and then adapt our skills to match these new definitions.

Here's the first reveal: if this process sounds somewhat familiar, it's because it has a much more common name – <u>learning</u>. The act of taking in, organizing, and acting upon knowledge in order to transfer skills between domains is the process of learning.

Here's the second reveal: earlier when I stated there is no 'all-purpose' skill directly applicable across any and every domain, I lied. It turns out there is one skill that, once mastered, can be applied anywhere and everywhere. Have you guessed what it is?

Learning.

Seeing as the process of learning is the means by which we enter into and come to understand new domains, the process itself is largely acontextual and unchanging. It doesn't matter if you wish to learn about the law, medicine, or accounting, the same three steps (knowledge, contextualization, adaptation) are essential.

This means that the only unequivocal way to prepare students for an unpredictable future is to empower them with agency over the learning process. Furthermore, those who know how to learn will be the first to determine relevant knowledge, define relevant skills, and adapt relevant standards within emerging fields. In other words, effective learners will set the bar for C21 skills in the future.

SO NOW THEN...

Although arguments have been made that explicitly teaching creativity, critical thinking, collaboration, and communication is a waste of time (especially with reference to the hurdle of contextualization outlined above), this debate is secondary to the far more important issue of transfer. How do we ensure students deeply understand the learning process so they can effectively move skills between contexts?

Despite decades of research, we've yet to uncover a shortcut through learning. The fundamental three-step progression must always be followed, which means there are only two useful suggestions to be made:

1. Be Explicit

2. Be Practised

Nearly all decisions teachers make are driven by a deep understanding of learning. Unfortunately, this understanding is too often buried within activities that require students to intuit the underlying pattern. This process of osmosis rarely works, and many students leave school without ever overtly knowing how to learn. In fact, an estimated 50% of high-performing high school students fail classes during their first semester of university. The reason isn't that they lack competence; it's that they don't know how to undertake the learning process without teacher support.

Accordingly, it's important the learning process is made *explicit*. For students to take agency over their learning, they must see behind the curtain of pedagogical decisions and internalize the vocabulary and patterns of learning. Employing questions like 'Where have we seen this material before?'; 'Why do you think we're starting today with a quick quiz?'; 'How is this similar to or different from what we learned last week?'; 'What previously learned skills might be relevant here?'; and 'What stage of learning are we up to now?' can help demystify the process and facilitate transfer.

Additionally, like all skills, mastering the process of learning requires time and effort. This means it must be frequently *practised* across varying contexts. Once students begin to recognize the same process occurring within all domains, they will gradually take increasing agency over that process. However, it's worth remembering that even with mastery, periods of struggle will still arise (such as my old driving habits rearing up when stressed). Fortunately, with a deep understanding of learning, these periods of struggle are rarely personalized. Instead, mistakes become a highly predictable part of the process, with minimal impact on self-worth or confidence.

As a final point, it's important to note that learning is different from study strategies. Many programmes, courses, and educational gurus focus on giving students tips and tricks to improve revision. Although well meaning, this has very little impact on behaviour. In fact, studies have demonstrated that although more than 90% of older students can easily differentiate between good and bad study techniques, fewer than 35% actually adhere to this advice. Why? Because knowing that a strategy exists tells you nothing about why it's useful, when it's meaningful, or how to adapt it across contexts. Study strategies only become meaningful when they are embedded within a deeper comprehension of the learning process.

In the end, there's no doubt that the four 21st century skills of creativity, critical thinking, collaboration, and communication are integral to thriving in the modern era. Frankly, these four skills have been integral to thriving in *every* era since humans first stood upright. However, we must recognize and remember that these competencies are highly contextual and will not automatically transfer across domains. Effective skill transfer requires a period of targeted and specific learning. Accordingly, making the learning process explicit and frequently practising this process across multiple domains is the best way to help students take agency over transfer and move important skills beyond the classroom.

CHAPTER 7

COMPUTERS – THE PROBLEM WITH PRIMARY FUNCTION

"HUMANITY IS ACQUIRING ALL THE RIGHT TECHNOLOGY FOR ALL THE WRONG REASONS."
– R. BUCKMINSTER FULLER

Burden of proof.

In a perfect world, this logical obligation ensures any individual making a claim is shouldered with the responsibility of proving that claim. This elevates established knowledge over proposed knowledge in order to protect people from being swept away by the slew of novel ideas propagated each day.

In law, this means accusers must demonstrate grievance: defendants need never prove they *did not* commit a crime. In medicine, this means pharmaceuticals must demonstrate efficacy: clinicians need never prove drugs *do not* alleviate symptoms. In education, this means tools must demonstrate positive impact: teachers need never prove tools *do not* improve learning.

Of course, we do not live in a perfect world.

Too often in law, public opinion shifts the burden of proof back to the defendant, leading to wrongful convictions. Too often in medicine, economic incentives shift the burden of proof back to the clinician, leading to unnecessary patient suffering. Too often in education, external hype shifts the burden of proof back to the teacher, leading to impaired learning.

Nowhere in education has this shift been more blatant than with the adoption of computers and internet technologies.

In a recent international survey, 92% of students reported having access to a computer at school. In New Zealand, 99.7% of schools are equipped with high-speed internet, while in Australia the computer-to-student ratio has dipped below 1:1 (meaning there are more computers than students in school). In the US, yearly expenditure on K–12 learning software exceeds $8 billion annually, while in the UK each school spends an average of £400,000 on computers every year.

With these numbers, you'd think the burden of proof had been met and that evidence demonstrating the beneficial impact of computers on learning had been clearly established.

Think again.

A 2015 OECD international review of the impact of computers in education states:

> *The results show no appreciable improvements in student achievement in reading, mathematics, or science in countries that had invested heavily in [computers] for education... Students who use computers very frequently at school do a lot worse in most learning outcomes... And perhaps the most disappointing finding of the report is that technology is of little help in bridging the skills divide between advantaged and disadvantaged students.*

After reviewing 126 research studies exploring technology-based education interventions, the global research centre J-PAL concluded:

> *Initiatives that expand access to computers... do not improve K–12 grades and test scores. [Furthermore], online courses lower student academic achievement compared to in-person courses.*

Recently, Larry Cuban, Emeritus Professor of Education at Stanford University and educational technology researcher for over 30 years, summed up the state of affairs:

> *The introduction of computers into schools was supposed to improve academic achievement and alter how teachers taught. Neither has occurred.*

In the references for this book, I have listed 50 'negative' research studies that demonstrate that computers and internet technologies significantly impair learning compared to traditional teaching methods.

Lest you think I'm cherry-picking, I have also listed 50 highly cited 'positive' research studies. Importantly, if you look closely, you'll notice 22 of these studies merely demonstrate that computers *do not harm* learning (they have the same impact as traditional teaching methods), while 13 of the remaining studies only compare computers to baseline data. This suggests that a full 70% of studies frequently cited to argue for the inclusion of computers in education do not show that computers enhance learning.

Imagine if, after deliberating a court case, a set of jurors voted six for innocent, four for abstain, and only two for guilty. There isn't a judge alive who would sentence a defendant under these circumstances.

Imagine if, after a series of clinical trials, a new pharmaceutical was found to worsen symptoms 50% of the time, have no impact 35% of the time, and only improve symptoms 15% of the time. This drug would never see the light of day.

Imagine if, after 100 research studies, an educational tool was shown to impair learning half the time, be no better than traditional teaching methods over half the remaining time, and improve learning in fewer than two out of every 10 attempts...

The fact that robust evidence has done little to quell the excitement over educational technology suggests that this is not an issue of efficacy. Rather, this is an issue of identity.

Just like gun control, climate change, and vaccinations, this topic likely won't be decided by research and must be tackled at a more fundamental level.

THE BIG ISSUE

It might come as no surprise, but the primary function of a tool is largely dictated by how individuals most often utilize that tool. For instance, if I were to hand you a hammer, you would almost certainly look for a nail to hit. This is not because a hammer can't be used for other purposes; it's because the primary function of a hammer has long been established through previous use and experience.

So, what is the primary function of a computer? A recent survey exploring how over 1500 students around the US aged 8–18 most often utilize this tool provides the answer (values below are per week):

- 10 hours 44 minutes playing video games

- 10 hours 2 minutes watching television or film clips

- 8 hours 14 minutes scrolling social media

- 7 hours 32 minutes listening to music

- 3 hours 25 minutes doing homework

- 2 hours 5 minutes doing schoolwork

- 1 hour 14 minutes reading for pleasure

- 52.5 minutes creating digital content

- 14 minutes writing for pleasure

(Tasks listed above are not always done in isolation: ~30% of computer time is spent multitasking.)

Do you see the issue?

Students spend over 32.5 hours each week using computers to jump between various forms of media and entertainment. This is nearly 6 times more than the 5.5 hours they spend using computers for learning. Include the fact that schools are in session only 180 days per year, and this means that of the nearly 2224 hours (93 days) students spend on a computer each year, less than 9% of that time is used for learning purposes.

This is why, when using a computer for homework, students typically last less than 6 minutes before accessing social media, messaging friends, and engaging with other digital distractions. This is why, when using a laptop during class, students typically spend 38 minutes of every hour off task. This is why, even while getting *paid* as part of a research study to focus on a 20-minute computerized lesson, nearly 40% of students were unable to stop themselves from multitasking.

It's not that modern students have abnormally short attention spans or weak constitutions. It's that when students sit in front of a computer they have thousands of hours of previous use and experience dictating that the primary function is to passively consume rapidly shifting media content.

Don't get me wrong; I am not arguing that computers *can't* be used for learning. I am arguing that they so often *aren't* used for learning, and that trying to shoehorn in this function puts a very large (and very unnecessary) obstacle between the student and the desired outcome. In order to effectively learn while using a computer, students must expend an incredible amount of cognitive effort battling impulses they've spent years developing – a battle they frequently lose. Furthermore, the energy spent trying to inhibit primary behaviours is necessarily energy not spent focusing on learning.

This is akin to sitting a group of alcoholics around a jug of beer and asking them to use it for learning about buoyancy. It's not that beer can't be used for this purpose (and individuals who have never before come across this drink will have no problem using it in this manner), it's that alcoholics have a deeply embedded story concerning the primary function of beer. As such, in order to undertake the learning, these individuals will have to expend continuous and conscious effort fighting temptation and quelling their instincts. In the end, even if they manage to avoid taking the drink, chances are they will have learned a thing or two about impulse control, but very little about buoyancy.

It's worth mentioning that, even without computers, students naturally struggle with lack of attention, shallow thinking, overconfidence, and other inimical learning behaviours. However, with computers, the likelihood of these behaviours is far greater. Seeing as many schools already struggle with engagement, why would we voluntarily throw a tool into the mix that exacerbates this problem while simultaneously harming (or, at best, not helping) the ultimate goal of learning?

THE THREE APOLOGIES

Despite the fact that neither the data nor the primary function of computers favours their use as a learning tool, enthusiasts still maintain that computers are the answer education has been seeking. Apologist arguments typically revolve around three primary themes.

Apology #1: *Computers have so much potential.*

It's easy to get swept up in the promise of computers in education. Returning to the J-PAL review quoted earlier, after concluding that computers largely harm learning, this group goes on to state:

> Computer assisted learning shows considerable _promise_... *against this backdrop, promising uses of education technology have the _potential_ to support massive inroads in learning.*

This is the apology that, intentionally or not, shifts the burden of proof.

Potential is what something could be, what it should be, what it ought to be – not what it actually is. This means arguments for potential are not arguments from fact and they do not accurately reflect reality. Instead, they reflect faith, belief, and desire.

When potential is promoted above reality, individuals are unfairly tasked with disproving a fantasy. If you've ever had to convince a sports fanatic that their basement-dwelling team is no good, then you'll recognize that disproving a fantasy is impossible. No matter how much negative evidence accrues, potential will always remain unblemished because it exists in the mind, not on the ground.

I am not arguing against having faith in computers; there is every possibility that someone will eventually invent a digital program that outperforms even the best of teachers. I am simply pointing out that this has not yet happened, and that promissory arguments are not a solid enough foundation upon which to settle issues of education.

Luckily, this apology is easily circumvented by shifting the burden of proof back to its proper location. Schools and teachers should only be asked to consider adopting computers and internet technologies when it has been unequivocally demonstrated that they can significantly improve learning – not when a group of people *believes* they should.

Apology #2: *Computers are ubiquitous.*

Driving. Health insurance. Alcohol. Taxes. Video games. Dating, marriage, and divorce. Mortgages. Laundry. Student loans. Pregnancy. Litigation. Television. Starting a business. Stock investments. Raising children. Criminal records. Rent. Hygiene. Sex. Table manners. Smoking. Retail sales. Moving home. Lego. Job applications and interviews. Self-defence. Negotiations. First aid. Pet care. Hiring employees. Superannuation.

I mention these things to highlight that just because something is ubiquitous does not mean it need be explicitly taught in school. Teachers have long recognized that they are not alone in the journey of education, and that many essential ideas are meant to be passed along by parents, peers, society, and life experience.

With that said, an argument could easily be made that schools should be teaching these ubiquitous subjects – that it's the responsibility of education to ensure all students are well versed in those things they are certain to encounter in their adult lives.

Honestly, this is a compelling argument with some merit.

However, to argue that a topic *should be taught* is far different from arguing that all things should be taught *through that topic*. The first is an argument about curriculum, the second is an argument about pedagogy. For instance, you might believe we should teach table manners to students (curriculum), but that's different from arguing we should teach all classes in a dining room over dinner (pedagogy).

Here is where the ubiquity apology goes awry. Through some linguistic alchemy, the argument 'we should teach computer skills' has morphed into 'we should teach all skills through a computer'. This has led to an abundance of backward reasoning, such as this excerpt from a 2010 paper exploring the impact of 1:1 computer programs in education:

> *[There has been] a generation of criticism levelled at 1:1 laptop computer initiatives... We raise questions about what classrooms and schools need to look like in order to realize the advantages of 1:1 computing. In doing so, we present a theoretical vision for self-organizing schools in which laptop computers or other devices are essential tools.*

Notice that these authors are not arguing that 1:1 computing has proven effective in schools; they are arguing that schools need to be reconfigured *in order for* 1:1 computing to be effective. As to why it's so important that laptops become essential tools within education, the only conceivable answer is... because they exist!

Although teaching computer skills is a worthwhile goal, it does not follow that we must adapt all of education to achieve this goal. When it comes to effective teaching and learning, we should select the tool best suited to the job, not the tool that is most prevalent.

<u>Apology #3</u>: *Teachers and students are using computers incorrectly.*

It seems nobody is immune to this argument. As referenced earlier, following a three-year analysis of hundreds of thousands of data points and concluding that computers do not benefit learning, the OECD goes on to state:

One interpretation of all this is that building deep, conceptual understanding and higher-order thinking requires intensive teacher–student interaction... Another interpretation is that we have not yet become good enough at the kind of pedagogies that make the most of technology.

To argue that people are not using a tool correctly is merely to argue that they are not using it as the inventor intended. To understand why this apology is so flimsy, we need only return to Chapter 3, where Thamus (Socrates) warned:

[T]he inventor of an art is not always the best judge of the utility of that invention to the users of it.

Philo T. Farnsworth, inventor of the electronic television, *intended* his tool to disseminate knowledge of international culture in order to drive global understanding and peace. Of course, television quickly became a means to disseminate entertainment and market products (leading Farnsworth to ultimately ban television from his household).

Robert Propst, inventor of the action office, *intended* his easily reconfigurable office dividers to promote employee productivity, privacy, and health. Of course, the action office was quickly renamed the 'cubicle' and became a way to maximize office space while lowering employee satisfaction and output (leading Propst to ultimately denounce his invention as monolithic insanity).

Alfred Nobel, inventor of dynamite, *intended* his invention to be used only for industrial purposes and thought its incredible power would preclude it from being used in war. Of course, dynamite quickly became a source of military might and caused untold numbers of deaths (leading Nobel to establish his eponymous prize in promotion of peace).

There is no doubt the engineers and programmers working on educational hardware and software have very specific *intentions* for how their tools should be utilized. Ultimately, however, these intentions are inconsequential. Once a tool makes it into the hands of the populace, it is they who decide how it will (and will not) be utilized. The user is the ultimate determinant of function.

When over 90% of students spend over 90% of their computer time jumping between passively consumed media, we can rest assured that this is the correct way to use the tool. To blame students because they're not using the tool as the designer intended is no different from arguing from potential: fantasy must play second fiddle to reality.

In the interest of digging deeper, let's give this apology the benefit of the doubt. If computers are in fact being used incorrectly in schools, then what is the correct way to use them? As the OECD states:

> *[Internet and computer technology] is linked to better student performance...*
> *when computer software and internet connections help to increase study*
> *time and practice.*

In case you missed it, let me rephrase that: learning improves when students *spend more time learning.*

This revelation is not unique to computers. Flashcards, workbooks, whiteboards, an empty milk jug, a box of wet ferrets, my great aunt Justine: when used to increase study time and practice, literally any tool will improve student performance. The relevant question is whether or not computers actually *do* lead to increased learning time. Unfortunately, as we've already established, the answer to this is an unequivocal 'no'.

TEN MINOR APOLOGIES

Once the arguments for potential, ubiquity, and intention have been addressed, a plethora of minor apologies used by computer enthusiasts lose much of their lustre.

1. We need more time and research to determine how best to utilize
   computers.

This might be true. However, like all forms of nascent research, this work should begin with small, controlled groups. To demand that education at large participate in an uncertain experiment is to ask unwitting students and teachers to pay the price for an exploration based on desire. Only after it's clear that computers demonstrate a predictable and reliable learning benefit within smaller studies should we consider how to best scale this work throughout education.

2. Computers make learning fast.

The wealth of aforementioned research makes it clear that, when utilized for similar durations, computers by and large impair learning compared to traditional teaching methods. This means students must spend *more* time on computers, not less, to achieve comparable results. In addition, it's not clear that 'speed' has ever been a defining characteristic of learning. Effective learning often requires deliberate effort, thought, and practice; processes that each require time.

3. Computers make learning fun.

Although pleasure has been linked to motivation, the correlation between enjoyment and learning is surprisingly weak. Chances are you've sat through an incredibly enjoyable film that you remember little of today. Conversely, chances are you've sat through a confronting film that, thanks to subsequent discussions, you remember deeply today.

The issue of importance is not enjoyment, per se, but how this emotion is leveraged to drive engagement with effective learning practices. That computers may be fun is trivial. Does this fun lead students to undertake meaningful activities known to enhance learning? Unfortunately, the research suggests that this follow-on effect is not occurring.

4. Computers can help students develop 21st century skills.

As we explored in the previous chapter, to stay relevant in an increasingly automated world, 21st century citizens must hone those skills that are uniquely human. To this end, critical thinking, creativity, collaboration, and communication have been singled out as important because they are precisely those skills which computers cannot do well. Surely trying to use a computer to teach students how *not to think* like a computer is the same as trying to use water to drown a fish: in no way does the tool suit the purpose.

5. Computers are adaptive and can guide learning.

In order for educational computer programs to be adaptive, they must have a predetermined outcome – a correct answer that allows users to be incorrect, thereby triggering the adaptive process. Though this may be effective for surface knowledge, what happens when we wish to take learning deeper? It's one thing to correctly define the term 'atom', but it's quite another to debate whether or not this definition is clear and meaningful across all contexts, what beliefs led to the atom's discovery, or what the atom's equivalent might be across varied systems of thought.

Once learning progresses beyond binary outcomes, the a priori destinations demanded by computers become a hindrance. Rather than rigid adaptation driving a singular outcome, students require a deeply flexible form of adaptation that allows for ambiguity, ambivalence, and open-ended solutions. Luckily, teachers have been demonstrating this type of adaptability for centuries.

6. *Computers increase enrolment/decrease costs/improve profit margins.*

Though possibly true, this apology does not concern learning and is irrelevant to matters of the classroom. The same is true for arguments concerning ease of scheduling, contact, or assignment submission. Though these are all wonderful benefits supported by computers, they aren't learning considerations and should not be construed as such.

7. *Computers make it easy to collect and analyse data.*

Data is only meaningful when it can be utilized to serve a clear purpose. Unfortunately, the digital data many teachers are tasked with collecting (button clicks, time-on-page, video access statistics) is decontextualized, overwhelming, and incredibly difficult to parse. When data becomes so vast and nuanced as to require the use of a computer for its collection, analysis, visualization, and conceptualization, then it's time to question the function of this exercise.

On the other hand, when the purpose of educational data is made explicit (to guide pedagogy and learning), it becomes far easier to reorient towards that data which is meaningful and worth collecting.

8. *Computers allow access to a wealth of information.*

Approximately 90% of schools can boast possession of a library, meaning 'access to information' is not a problem that modern education has ever truly suffered from.

This apology picks up steam when it incorporates equity. More specifically, it's possible that computers can allow under-privileged students access to the same materials available to more privileged students. Though I strongly support the ideals of equity, remember the OECD statement quoted earlier: '...technology is of little help in bridging the skills divide between advantaged and disadvantaged students.'

If history has taught us anything, it's that the benefits of a technology are never equally distributed. Even among ubiquitous technologies like the automobile, air conditioning, and (indeed) the computer, there remains a tremendous gulf in quality and peripherals available to the rich versus the poor. Accordingly, if educational equity is the destination, then computers do not appear to be the route.

9. *Computers allow students to choose topics and create personal learning pathways.*

Love it or hate it, one of the primary functions of education has always been the coherent organization of information. Through what they include (and, of equal importance, what they exclude), curricula serve not only to inoculate students from information overload, but also to support learning by structuring content into a rational trajectory.

Without coherent organization, information loses context and becomes a source of confusion rather than a source of clarity. A natural response to this confusion is to focus only on those facts already well understood. This is why, when allowed to choose their own learning pathways, most students gravitate towards topics they are already deeply familiar with (sports, music, video games, etc.). It's not that they lack curiosity; it's that without proper guidance, students become overwhelmed by information chaos and meaning is lost.

When computers are used to reduce the capacity of schools to structure information, they do so at the expense of learner agency and growth.

10. *Computers allow students to access classes whenever and wherever.*

When schools mandate that teachers place lectures online for students to access at their convenience, they send the message that learning is of lesser importance than every other life event. Doctor's appointment? No problem. Hanging out with friends? Go ahead. Hung over? Stay in bed.

To understand the impact of this message, one need only look at the statistics for open online learning courses. Despite millions of worldwide registrations over the last decade, fewer than 5% of enrolled students have ever completed these digital programs. Even among students who pay for course credit, completion rates are below 50%. Why such abysmal outcomes? Because when education is adapted to the lifestyle of the student, rigour is stripped from the process and personal accountability plummets.

Schools need to treat learning as an event: something that students commit to and build their lives around (not vice versa). When education fails to prioritize, elevate, or revere learning, why should students?

Now, I fully recognize that some individuals have a legitimate reason for being unable to attend live classes. Importantly, this can be (and historically has been) successfully addressed on a case-by-case basis. There's no reason to dismantle educational composition to accommodate for the rare case; it's far more practical to deal with the exception when it arises, while keeping the larger composition intact.

SO NOW THEN...

For over a decade, I have been asking educators to provide unambiguous examples of when they successfully used computers to benefit student learning. In that time, three patterns have emerged.

First, when schools are required to close as a result of environmental disasters (e.g. poor air quality due to fires), sociological upheavals (e.g. unsafe political protests), or health risks (e.g. local epidemics or global pandemics), then teachers often have no choice but to employ distance education. In these instances, it is difficult to argue against the use of computers: any form of learning is better than no form of learning. With that said, the issues of digital distractions, diminished impact, and socioeconomic divide still persist during distance learning.

Second, computers can prove a godsend for individuals with specific learning disabilities. Students with auditory impairments can use computers to transcribe speech; students with motor impairments can use computers to type; students with visual impairments can use computers to alter text presentation, etc.

Though these benefits cannot be overstated, it's important to recognize that one person's scaffold can become another person's crutch. Quite often, students with no underlying disability will exploit computers to indulge personal learning preferences and avoid the often difficult process of learning. Accordingly, when disability is not a factor, teachers must determine when it's acceptable to cater to preference, and when computers hinder the push into more difficult, less fluent realms.

Third, computer simulation appears to be effective when practising motor skills that otherwise would be too difficult or dangerous to train for in 'real' life, for example, airline pilots practising mid-air emergency manoeuvres; surgeons practising invasive procedures; or Formula One drivers practising city-street courses.

However, though simulation may benefit motor skills, the same cannot be said for knowledge of facts, dates, events, etc. As an example, a Greek school in Australia recently invested in virtual reality so that students could learn to speak Greek by conversing with an adaptive avatar projected in front of a digital Acropolis. Though well meaning, there's a far more effective and adaptive technique proven to yield better results: have students converse with an actual Greek-speaking person (of which, you'd imagine, there would be several within a Greek school). Sure, chatting in front of the Acropolis is a nice touch, but it's unlikely that a primary impediment for students learning to speak a second language is the lack of nearby ancient architecture. When simulations transition from motor skills into declarative realms, the same learning issues that plague more traditional computer programs come into play.

In the end, it's been roundly demonstrated that computers, by and large, hinder learning. Once arguments for potential, ubiquity, and intention are abandoned, and computers are considered for what they are (rather than what we desire them to be), it becomes questionable whether or not digital technologies should continue to play such a large role in education. Moving forward, we must rationally debate the merits of all emerging tools and consider adopting only those that unambiguously demonstrate benefits to learning.

CHAPTER 8

REWARDS – THE PROBLEM WITH COERCION

"NO ONE ASKS HOW TO MOTIVATE A BABY. A BABY NATURALLY EXPLORES EVERYTHING IT CAN GET AT... AND THIS TENDENCY DOESN'T DIE, IT'S WIPED OUT."

– B.F. SKINNER

In his book *Predictably Irrational,* Duke University professor Dan Ariely reflects on the surprising findings from one of his experiments – an experiment that likely isn't mentioned in most teacher training courses.

This experiment involved participants undertaking a mundane, meaningless task. A circle was displayed on the left side of a computer screen, while a square was displayed on the right. The task was to use a mouse to drag the circle into the square, at which point a new circle would appear. Participants were given 5 minutes to drag across as many circles as possible.

Before commencing, some participants were paid 50c, while others were paid $5. Can you guess what happened? The individuals who received $5 dragged an average of 159 circles, while those who received 50c only dragged an average of 101 circles. This appears to be clear-cut proof that rewarding people can boost motivation and performance.

But here's the twist: some participants were paid *nothing*. Those individuals who received zero compensation dragged an average of 168 circles, which was significantly more than either of the participant groups that got paid!

In truth, this experiment suggests that rewarding people might actually *decrease* motivation and performance.

There is an explanation here – an important explanation that turns out to be quite profound when we consider the context of student motivation. To understand, let's first revisit the early days of human motivation science.

OF RATS AND MEN

Who is the most eminent psychologist of the 20th century? Is it Carl Jung? Abraham Maslow? Sigmund Freud?

According to a team of American psychologists, it's actually the infamous Harvard professor B.F. Skinner. A staunch adherent to the tenets of behaviourism, Skinner believed that free will was illusory and that human behaviour represents little more than a conditioned response to external stimuli. As such, he maintained that behaviours could be 'shaped' and 'chained together' in predictable ways using simple rewards and punishments.

Skinner's most notable set of experiments involved a conditioning chamber (commonly referred to as a Skinner Box). He showed that the behaviour of rats placed inside this chamber could quite easily and reliably be trained through the use of food pellets or electric shocks. The 'free will' of these animals, it seemed, was quite literally at the mercy of scientists holding a token snack.

Interesting. But humans aren't rats, right?

Enter Nathan Azrin.

Building upon Skinner's work, Azrin published research in 1968 demonstrating that adaptive, pro-social behaviours could actively be cultivated among psychiatric hospital patients in the same way that rat behaviour could be cultivated in the Skinner Box. In order to shape these behaviours, metal tokens were awarded to patients for performing favourable actions like washing dishes or assisting others at mealtimes. These tokens could later be exchanged for benefits like extra outdoor time or bonus cigarettes. Azrin's research was well received, and this 'token economy' model was soon adopted by prisons, hospitals, and schools around the world.

Good news for teachers: rewards can drive specific behaviours.

Not so fast. In all six of Azrin's experiments, the performance fell to a *near-zero level* when the established response reinforcement relation was discontinued. Put simply, as soon as Azrin stopped supplying patients with tokens, they went right back to acting as they had before. This extinction effect has since been replicated in dozens of studies; there is simply no compelling evidence for a sustained behavioural impact following the termination of a token economy.

Bad news for teachers: rewarded behaviour stops when the rewards stop.

Moreover, not only do external rewards lack staying power, but they also struggle to impact behaviour across varied situations. The psychological concept of <u>generalization</u> refers to the tendency of a person or animal to respond similarly to different but related stimuli. For example, in Pavlov's famous study, not only did his dogs salivate whenever they heard a bell, but they also salivated whenever they heard any sound resembling a bell.

Unfortunately, behaviours rewarded in a token economy do not effectively generalize. In fact, a number of educational studies dating back to the 1970s have shown that behaviours driven by rewards in one classroom rarely transfer to other classroom settings. In one such study, researchers lamented that although student behaviour was 'reliably affected by token reinforcement procedures [during morning sessions]... generalization of beneficial effects was not noted during the afternoon class in which token procedures were not in effect.' This means we can pay kids to behave in a certain way – but we must continue to pay them all day in every class.

Worse news for teachers: rewarded behaviour does not generalize across contexts.

To further compound matters, in 1942 researcher Leo Crespi found that rats could be coerced to run progressively faster by providing them with increasingly large food-based rewards. However, once he shifted from large rewards back to smaller rewards, then rats ran *even slower* than they did before rewards were ever introduced. Crespi attributed the significant performance decline that occurred after the rewards were downgraded to a 'manifestation of some degree of frustration [due to rewards being] below the level of expectation.' In other words, the rewards very quickly created heightened expectations which triggered performance crashes when those expectations were not met.

This phenomenon, called <u>behavioural contrast</u>, is equally manifest among humans. Once specific behaviours are incentivized at a certain level, those behaviours become inextricably linked to that level of incentive. Imagine how frustrated you would become if your boss suddenly started paying you 50% of your salary to do the same job. Imagine how frustrated students would become if one teacher handed out candy for a certain behaviour, while another teacher did not. In essence, discontinuing a reward is perceived as a form of punishment – meaning that once we start using rewards to motivate student behaviour, we can't stop.

Even worse news for teachers: rewarded behaviours decline when reward levels decline.

There is one final idea to consider. Currently, there are hundreds of schools in America where financial incentives are being used as a motivational tool. One major study examined the impact of paying 27,000 primary and middle school students a total of $9,400,000 to read and study. That's right – schools are literally paying kids to read. And the outcome? It was concluded that the '[long-term] impact of financial incentives on student achievement is statistically 0.' Even if rewards can guarantee an increase in desired behaviours like reading, they can't guarantee learning.

Decades of research across domains ranging from weight loss to anti-smoking have shown that intervention programmes that incentivize behavioural change through rewards can at best produce mildly positive gains in the short term, and at worst produce significantly negative impacts in the long term. In fact, there is so much evidence highlighting the detrimental impact that rewards can have on enduring performance that psychologists have coined the term undermining effect. Put simply, external or *extrinsic* rewards tend to 'undermine' any internal or *intrinsic* motivational sources such as joy, pleasure, or purpose that might typically drive behaviours.

We can certainly ply students with money or chocolate or grades to compel them to read, practise, and study. In the short term, these rewards might work well to drive particular behaviours. Unfortunately, once we consider the long-term consequences of using rewards, they quickly lose their appeal.

The worst news for teachers: rewards can harm long-term behaviours.

This begs the question: if rewards only work when they're incessantly dispensed, fail to demonstrate generalization, produce behavioural reversal when reduced, and undermine long-term performance and motivation, is there any justification for maintaining reward-based incentive systems in schools? Is there any reason to keep using certificates, aromatic stickers, grades, prizes, and trophies?

You bet there is – and it's a very big reason.

Compliance.

CUI BONO?

During my second year of teaching, I was allocated a Year 7 medieval European history class. At the same time, I was also teaching B.F. Skinner and Nathan Azrin to my Year 11 psychology students.

My Year 7s were a great group whom I enjoyed teaching immensely. But there were always a few students who would fail to complete the obligatory 15 minutes of homework each night. For this reason, I wanted to come up with something that would encourage everyone to engage with their work.

You know what's coming next, don't you?

In a kind of pedagogical mash-up, I created a token economy system whereby students would earn a sticker for each homework assignment they completed. If enough stickers were obtained across the entire class, they would win a teacher-funded pizza party. In order to turbo-charge this process, I leveraged another bit of the Year 11 psychology curriculum: social influence. Not only did *each* student need to collect stickers, but *all* students needed to achieve a near perfect homework record to earn enough stickers for the pizza party. Cue peer pressure.

Needless to say, we ate pizza.

Some people might be tempted to congratulate me on my creative teaching. Heck, I was able to get even the most stubborn of kids to complete their homework without a threat of punishments or reprimands – that's no small feat. Indeed, I remember being quite chuffed at the time.

Unfortunately, there's a lovely Latin phrase often used in legal contexts that has since caused me to reinterpret this episode: *Cui bono?* Roughly translated, it means *to whom is it a benefit?* In other words, *who wins?*

When I use rewards and peer pressure to coerce teenagers into completing medieval history homework assignments that they neither enjoy nor are particularly interested in, *cui bono?* When I dole out grades, stickers, or shiny certificates as a means to compel students to study harder and get the right answers on exams, *who wins?*

One way to interpret my pizza experiment is to believe that it was the students who benefitted. Not only did they get free pizza, but they also completed important work that supported their learning, enriched their education, and enhanced their future prospects.

If only it were that simple.

Sure, it's possible that there were some (albeit not many) students who, because of my reward system, initially engaged with the homework to avoid any shame or guilt associated with non-completion. And sure, it's possible that some (albeit not many) of these students continued to engage with the homework out of a personal sense of responsibility. And sure, it's even possible that over time, some (albeit not many) of these students came to incorporate this newly found work ethic into their larger self-concept. Unfortunately, this idealized progression is incredibly rare, and it does not confer the beneficial impact many people would assume.

Most teachers use rewards merely as a means to open a doorway. The objective is for students to walk through this doorway and eventually assume autonomy over their own learning process. This isn't irrational thinking. In fact, psychologists Richard Ryan and Ed Deci have developed a related framework called <u>organismic integration theory,</u> which explains how it is possible for extrinsically motivated behaviours to evolve from 'internalization' to 'identification' to 'integration'. Once integration is achieved, we end up with students who actively choose to do homework – not because it is compulsory, but because it aligns with their identity.

The problem is that even when reward-driven behaviours are fully integrated into our identity, they never truly become intrinsically motivating. In other words, just because we assume agency over a rewarded behaviour does not mean we will ever truly be passionate about or derive fulfilment from that behaviour.

For example, consider my colleague Simon. Simon has a military background which has led him to always arrive early for meetings and appointments. As he once quipped, 'If you're five minutes early, you're late.' Whereas being punctual was originally drilled into him through training, he has come to integrate this behaviour into his larger identity.

However, Simon doesn't enjoy the process of being early. He doesn't derive satisfaction getting up for work at 5:30 a.m. He doesn't find meaning in setting out his breakfast items before going to bed. He does these things because they align with his sense of personal obligation – but they do not motivate, drive, or inspire him as a truly intrinsic passion would.

I applaud Simon, just as I applaud any student who develops personal agency over homework completion. But as Ryan and Deci explain, behaviours that have become integrated via rewards are not maintained because they are inherently interesting, satisfying, or meaningful. They are maintained because, post-integration, there remains a sense of reward through the fulfilment of a personal obligation. Put simply, the reward never disappears, it merely becomes internalized (which also explains why any time a personal obligation is not met, an internal sense of punishment will be felt).

To make matters worse, this process of internalization is quite atypical. What about the majority of students who will never integrate the many rewarded behaviours prevalent in education? With them, we're stuck with the problems outlined above of extinction, generalization, behavioural contrast, and undermining.

So, *cui bono?*

In the case of my pizza experiment, aside from those few who were able to successfully integrate homework behaviour (even though they still may not like it), it appears my students did not benefit. In the end, the only winner was...me.

My approach was a classic example of what writer Alfie Kohn describes as 'doing to' rather than 'working with'. Undoubtedly, I was exercising my power in order to get less powerful humans to do something I wanted them to do. I had a curriculum to get through (my most hated phrase in education), and so I used rewards to engender compliance among those who had no meaningful say in the matter.

While this system of compliance was grounded in good intentions, it was nonetheless manipulative. Fortunately, it worked: we got through the curriculum. The homework was completed, *my* students got good marks, *my* annual review was strong, and *my* goal was achieved. I benefitted.

But here's the thing; whenever I bump into former students and we reminisce about the past, there is never even a hint of cynicism or anger on their part. So I can justify my actions. Yes, the rewards probably didn't enhance overall learning. Yes, my students stopped doing homework when the rewards stopped.

Yes, performance and motivation were likely wounded in the long run. And yes, I used power to coerce behaviour. But my students all came out fine; some of them learned new material, some of them internalized good habits, and all of them ate pizza.

And yet, for some reason, this justification seems to me the worst part of all. Simply because my students 'came out all right' does not indicate that my coercion was harmless or meaningless. In truth, small nudges used to drive behaviour remain very important for two interrelated reasons.

WHAT'S THE BIG DEAL?

First, behavioural nudges penetrate deep inside our students' brains.

Neuroscientists studying rewards have begun to map the brain circuitry associated with reward-driven behaviour. When a teacher attaches a reward to a behaviour or outcome, this directly impacts future value computations processed within the student's ventromedial prefrontal cortex. Rewards nudge our behaviour largely by guiding the brain (which almost always seeks the most beneficial outcome) down a clearly marked path. Once a reward is received, it feels good, increases the value computation, and is more likely to be positively judged by the brain in the future.

Put simply, whenever we use rewards to control student behaviour, we are literally shaping their neural representations of value – both immediately and into the future.

Which brings us to the second reason why behavioural nudges matter: they transmit our social values.

Rewards, like rules and consequences, are values in practice. Why must we stop at a red traffic light even when we're running late for work? Because, as a society, we value collective safety over individual punctuality. Why are only first-time home buyers eligible for a governmental cash incentive? Because, as a group, the government values supporting those with fewer resources over supporting a completely free market. Why is it that recreational marijuana use is legal in many American states but illegal in all Australian states? Because, as a nation, Australians value sending a strong anti-drug message over reducing the illegal drug trade. There's no right or wrong here – but rewards are never random; rather, they clearly reflect and transmit an underlying value structure.

We reward what we value, and students learn to value what we reward.

So, what do we reward?

VALUE THIS

School has always been a 'gamified' system. Just like in all games, there are rules, stages, checkpoints, patterns, and strategies. Some students win; doors open and pathways are lit. Some students lose; doors close and the pathways go dark. But it's particularly in the last 30 years, as university entry has become more desirable and more competitive, that this gamification has ramped up.

Q. *How do I win at school?*

A. Outscore the other students on assignments and exams.

Q. *How do I outscore others?*

A. Do what the system expects of you.

This is the game of school – a game that pivots on two axes: competition and compliance. When we perpetuate this game, these are the values we espouse.

Schools that embrace prizes invariably reward competition and compliance. Students win by outperforming their peers at learning, sport, music, even effort. Schools that embrace bell curves invariably reward competition and compliance. Students who top the list need not perform absolutely well; they need only outperform their peers.

We can emblazon the highest-minded mottos on the most beautifully designed school crests, but it is through our rewards that we primarily transmit our values (and, by extension, transmit to our students what they should value).

Are the values of competition and compliance really what we hold dear? Are these the values that get teachers out of bed in the morning? Are these the values we truly hope to instil in our students?

For many, the answer to these questions is a resounding no. Luckily, there is an alternative.

SO NOW THEN...

An approach based on competition and compliance has major advantages when there exists a scarcity of resources, such as when there's not enough food, shelter, or energy to go around. In a zero-sum game, behaviours naturally become geared to winning and losing, and so too do rewards.

This suggests that a scarcity mindset underpins the competitive, extrinsic incentivisation system inherent in traditional schooling. Accordingly, schools have become a fertile environment for what renowned management consultant John Hagel refers to as the 'masculine archetype': a way of thinking that prioritises short-term goals; a transactional approach to interactions (*What can I get out of this?*); the accumulation and hoarding of knowledge and power; and the exploitation of any and every advantage.

Some educators vehemently believe that we must continue to reward competition and compliance because they represent the natural and enduring conditions of the *real world*.

However, the real world has always proved to be much more adaptive. Throughout human history, when scarcity has given way to abundance, very interesting things have happened.

For instance, take our early ancestors: when hunter/gatherer tribes gave way to agrarian societies, food became abundant and humans began working together to make incredible strides in art, technology, literature, and astronomy. Or consider the space race: when militant competition gave way to international cooperation, great advances in space technology became possible, culminating in the development of the International Space Station (a truly astonishing marvel of human ingenuity).

The same type of evolution is possible in education. When students stop battling over artificially limited 'A' grades, academic awards, and scarce university spots, then compliance and competition fade away. In their place will emerge empathy, compassion, teamwork, and meaningful innovation – both among students and teachers.

When scarcity gives way to abundance, we can embrace the 'feminine archetype'. As Hagel explains, our mind and energies turn outwards, and we focus more on high-quality, long-term relationships and less on immediate, transactional interactions. We seek to more deeply understand the world and our place within it. And, perhaps most importantly, we embrace change because it provides a powerful catalyst for growth and learning.

This is a world of intrinsic motivation – where learning is powered not by rankings or rewards, but by a desire to contribute meaningfully through our humanity. This is a classroom where rewards still exist, but where they are inherent in the learning rather than appended by the teacher.

Unfortunately, intrinsic motivation is difficult to embrace in a classroom. Teachers can't create, cause, or coerce it – they can only cultivate it. Intrinsic motivation emerges only when an activity or behaviour feels like it makes sense – like it genuinely matters. When this occurs, we can put away the awards and dispense with the bell curves.

Even among individuals with no specific dreams or desires, intrinsic motivation can emerge with clear evidence of impact. When people undertake tasks that deliver unambiguous benefits to the wider world, most can't help but engage deeply. For instance, when students work to solve the littering problem at the local park, or are asked to produce a public service YouTube video, or serve as a mentor to younger students, intrinsic motivation can't help but increase.

Think back to a moment in your life when learning felt good, made sense, and mattered. A gold star or a $20 bill likely wouldn't have made that experience more powerful. In fact, it may have only served to cheapen the experience.

Within schools that depend heavily on extrinsic rewards, the shift to internal motivation might require a slow, strategic weaning process. While this occurs (or where external rewards remain unavoidable), there are a few ideas that might help to minimise negative impact:

- Ensure that rewards are clearly linked to a desired behaviour and not diffused among many behaviours. As much as possible, we want students to recognize and focus on the adaptive behaviour – not the reward itself.

- Apply rewards as quickly as possible after the desired behaviour is observed. When rewards are left 'dangling', not only does this reduce effectiveness, but it also shifts focus toward the reward itself (as students won't always see the reward as linked to a distant behaviour).

- Give rewards intermittently rather than every time the desired behaviour is observed. Intermittent rewards not only increase efficacy, but also reduce reward expectations, thereby possibly assisting with the weaning process.

- Don't make students compete for rewards. By unnecessarily creating 'winners' and 'losers', this can lead to a number of negative consequences (including peer resentment and relationship issues).

This is not an argument for free-for-all learning: teachers will always be required to structure and assist the student journey through the learning trajectory. Nobody becomes an expert swimmer by jumping aimlessly into the deep end of a pool.

With that said, there is good cause to reconsider the particular practice of using rewards in education. Rewards should not be our default motivational tool. Rather, we should first seek to catalyse meaning and responsibility, and tap into the deep well of intrinsic motivation. If we get this right, we can activate a new type of drive within our students – one that embraces the tribe and works toward a collective betterment.

CHAPTER 9

ORGANIZATION – THE PROBLEM WITH STRUCTURE

"TIME IS WHAT WE WANT MOST, BUT WHAT WE USE WORST."
– WILLIAM PENN

In a 1784 letter to the *Journal de Paris*, Benjamin Franklin describes a shocking discovery: namely, that the sun rises earlier in summer months than it does in winter months. Extrapolating this astonishing finding, Franklin calculates that Parisians could save an incredible amount of energy each year if they simply woke with the sun and replaced artificial candle wax with all-natural daylight.

Of course, Franklin was being ironic (as evidenced by the fact that he also suggests taxing people who use shutters to block morning sunlight), but little did he recognize how prescient this satire would be.

At the peak of World War I (132 years later), Germany was looking for ways to conserve rapidly decreasing energy reserves. Their solution: institute a temporary scheme called 'daylight saving time'. Starting on 30 April 1916, all Germans and Austrians turned their clocks ahead by one hour so as to harness the sun, reduce artificial lighting, and conserve precious fossil fuels for military use. Britain, France, Russia and the United States quickly followed suit.

At the conclusion of the war, this scheme was internationally abandoned – only to be reintroduced during the global energy crisis of the 1970s. Unlike before, however, after this crisis abated, daylight saving wasn't abandoned and has remained a feature of calendars worldwide for nearly 50 years.

This wonderfully illustrates how a time-based organizational structure can be adopted to address a specific problem, yet persist long after that problem has been resolved. Daylight saving time was instituted to decrease energy consumption during periods of lack, yet continues despite most participating countries no longer struggling to keep the lights on. To make matters worse, there is now compelling evidence that daylight saving time actually *increases* energy consumption through the use of at-home air conditioners to combat warm evening hours.

This same pattern can be seen elsewhere. For example, the 8-hour working day was instituted to protect exploited workers from prolonged industrial work. This practice remains despite nearly 60% of modern work being knowledge-based (rather than manual labour) and reams of evidence demonstrating increased productivity, efficiency, and wellbeing with 6-hour working days. Similarly, the 3.5-minute pop song was instituted when radio stations began exclusively playing cheap 7-inch 45 rpm records (which can hold only about 4 minutes of music). This practice continues despite modern technology allowing for limitless music recording and dissemination.

Don't misunderstand: I have nothing against daylight saving time, the 8-hour working day, or 3.5-minute songs. I'm merely pointing out that once the historic function for a practice becomes obsolete, it's reasonable to re-examine that practice and determine whether or not it addresses modern issues. If the answer is 'no', then there is cause to discuss alternative practices which may be better suited to modern-day aims.

Schools are rife with time-based organizational practices that have long since outlived their historic function. Although the specifics differ somewhat between countries, the last century of Western education has broadly adhered to:

- 9-month school year/3-month summer vacation
- 50-minute class periods
- 8:00 a.m. start time.

Let's examine each of these organizational elements to determine if they align with modern goals of student learning.

9-MONTH/3-MONTH

Where did it come from?

For over two centuries (1684–1884), US public schooling was a year-round endeavour. During this period, Boston schools operated 244 days per year, New York schools ran 248 days, and Philadelphia schools were open 251 days.

It's commonly believed that the shorter school calendar was adopted for agrarian purposes; that school-free summers allowed kids to work the family farm. However, as many growers will attest, summer is hardly peak farming season. Seeing as most major crops are sown in the spring and reaped in the fall, a truly agrarian school calendar would only run during the summer and winter months.

In truth, the 9-month school year was an urban invention. In the late 19th century, the rate of people moving into cities far outpaced the amount of available work. In order to free up jobs for adults, it became necessary to remove kids from the workforce. This put a premium on school attendance: if kids were behind a desk, they couldn't be on the factory floor.

Unfortunately, at this time, school attendance was wildly inconsistent. On any given day, 25 to 35% of students wouldn't show up for school, with the worst attendance rates occurring during the summer, when many families would escape the fetid city heat by travelling to cooler climes (slow journeys that could last months). In order to lure students to the classroom, urban schools reduced the number of in-class days to 180 and instituted a 3-month break during summer to allow for extended family travel.

Now that we understand the reasoning behind the 9-month school year, we are free to ask if these reasons remain meaningful today.

The fact that mandatory school attendance laws are now extant in nearly all countries, that widely available air conditioning effectively combats fetid city heat, and that affordable air travel has reduced the average family vacation to only two weeks, it's safe to say the historic function of the 9-month school year is well and truly past its use-by date. Accordingly, we are in the clear to scrutinize this organizational habit from a learning perspective.

Is it good for learning?

The relevant cognitive issue to consider here concerns <u>forgetting</u>.

There is a phenomenon called *the forgetting curve* which suggests human beings forget 70 to 80% of new material within a month of learning it. Luckily, there is a way to combat this detrimental curve: it's called *spaced repetition*. Put simply, when newly learned material is recalled and interacted with over subsequent days or weeks, rapid memory decline can be greatly abated.

During the school year, students frequently undertake pop quizzes, review sessions, and discussion forums which serve as spaced repetition and largely work to keep the forgetting curve at bay.

Unfortunately, during the summer holidays, students rarely undertake pop quizzes, review sessions, or discussion forums. This means much content learned in the latter months of school won't undergo spaced repetition and is likely to be forgotten. In fact, the 'summer slump' is a well-documented occurrence whereby students regress about 30 days in their learning over the course of summer.

With that said, there is a wealth of evidence demonstrating that holidays can support memory by allowing students to rest and relax. Importantly, research suggests optimal recuperation is achieved by the 8th day of any vacation.

Combined, these ideas suggest that constructing the school year around a single, long-form vacation might not be the best organization for student learning. Rather, interspersing the traditional school year with frequent, short-term holidays may prove a better fit for learning.

What's the evidence?

Although some people argue we should add additional days to the school calendar, there appears to be little correlation between year length and performance on standardized measures of learning. In fact, among the 20 top-performing countries on the latest international PISA exam, school years range from 180 days (Poland) to 240 days (Taiwan), with an average of 193 days. Importantly, among the 20 bottom-performing countries, school years range from 180 days (Panama) to 240 days (Indonesia), with an average of 192 days. Nearly identical.

This suggests that the issue of importance here is not the number of days per school year, but rather how these days are organized.

Many schools have begun experimenting with year-round calendars modelled around shorter, more frequent breaks. The most common year-round organization is the 45/15, whereby students attend school for 9 weeks followed by a 3-week holiday (with traditional local and national holidays still observed).

Several meta-analyses have demonstrated that student learning in these year-round schools increases at the rate of about 1 month per year. Whereas some rightly point out that this is a small gain, it actually makes perfect sense. Remember: year-round schools do not increase learning time – they simply inoculate against the 'summer slump'. Seeing as this slump is equivalent to 1 month of learning, it shouldn't be a surprise to see students gain that month back in a year-round setting.

This leads to an important question: if schools choose to adopt a new learning calendar, will they also need to consider adopting a new learning day?

THE 50-MINUTE HOUR

Where did it come from?

At the turn of the 20th century, US higher education was a miscellany of institutions with little admissions coherence. For instance, to apply for Harvard, students were required to demonstrate proficiency in Latin, Greek, world geography, world history, planar geometry, and trigonometry. By contrast, to apply for Iowa State, students were merely required to prove they were at least 14 years old and demonstrate basic English and arithmetic skills.

Retired steel magnate cum philanthropist Andrew Carnegie changed all this.

In 1905, Carnegie established a $10 million pension fund for university professors. However, seeing as higher education was a hodgepodge, Carnegie was forced to set some criteria. In order to be considered an official 'university', an institution had to enrol only students who successfully completed 24 *Carnegie Units* – a brand new way to standardize learning, with each Carnegie Unit defined as 120 hours of instruction devoted to a single topic.

With $10 million on the line, uptake was swift, and universities began demanding prospective students complete their Carnegie Units for entry. Almost overnight, secondary schools became four-year institutions that devoted 120 hours to 6 different topics each year. Extrapolated, this organization equates to six 50-minute lessons per day over the course of 30 weeks.

This means the 50-minute class period that has characterized secondary education in Western countries for over a century was born from a cash-grab amongst American university professors. To make matters worse, Carnegie settled upon his eponymous 120-hour unit as a means to 'improve the administration efficiency of schools and colleges in the spirit of the "scientific management" movement of the day.'

Seeing as the 50-minute period was devised for administrative purposes, let's see what happens when we scrutinize this organizational feature through the lens of learning.

Is it good for learning?

The relevant cognitive issue to consider here is <u>processing power</u>.

As we learned in Chapter 6, the brain possesses a unique dual-system apparatus that shifts between active engagement and passive automaticity. In order to learn anything new, we must explicitly engage with that material (active). However, the more we experience and practise this material, the more we can subconsciously access it (passive).

Much of the time, the brain exists in passive mode and draws its energy from glucose: a simple sugar carried by the blood. However, whenever the brain flips into active mode, it requires more energy than blood can supply. Accordingly, when actively learning, it's believed the brain draws energy from *astrocytic glycogen*: a form of glucose stored in non-neuronal regions of the brain.

It's important to clarify that the energy-sapping active learning apparatus only activates when we undertake *new* learning or engage with highly difficult tasks. When we revise previously learned material or practise previously learned skills, the brain often need not tap into this secondary energy source.

Unfortunately, there's a problem: the brain can only hold a finite amount of astrocytic glycogen, meaning there is a limit to the amount of time the brain can spend actively learning. So, how long do we have?

Although astrocytic glycogen stores vary depending upon a number of biological factors, it's estimated people have anywhere between 30 minutes and several hours' worth of this fuel per day (replenished each night during sleep). Being generous, this suggests students will be able to spend approximately 3 hours each day actively engaging with new material before they reach cognitive fatigue and mentally burn out.

To compound matters, once the brain enters active learning mode, performance doesn't remain consistently strong; rather, performance tends to decrease with sustained effort. For instance, it has been suggested that students who study for 60 minutes remember only 9% more than students who study the same material for 30 minutes; nowhere near the double one would intuitively expect. Similarly, a number of studies exploring the difference between longer (60-minute) and shorter (<45-minute) secondary school class periods consistently reveal no significant difference in learning or comprehension.

When we combine the cognitive cost of active learning with the problem of diminishing returns, we see inklings that perhaps class periods should be shorter.

Importantly, there is a second relevant cognitive issue to consider: <u>flow state</u>.

Flow state (also called 'being in the zone') is a psychological phenomenon whereby individuals become deeply absorbed in a particular task and lose self-conscious awareness. During flow state, engagement increases, confidence grows, and productivity soars. If you've ever become so focused while gardening, playing a game, or cooking a meal that several hours flew by without you noticing, then you've experienced flow.

Although debate remains, it's believed flow state does *not* require astrocytic glycogen and, rather, subsists off blood glucose. This means individuals could conceivably remain in a flow state all day without reaching cognitive fatigue.

In order to attain flow, however, there are several requisites. First, it only occurs when performing a task that is deeply familiar but challenging (meaning flow will likely only arise during periods of practice, not learning). Second, it only occurs when undertaking a task that is intrinsically motivating (meaning flow can't be coerced using rewards and must emerge from personal desire). Third, it only occurs when undertaking a task for an extended period of time (meaning flow usually requires at least 30 minutes of focused effort before kicking in).

Considering flow state, we see inklings that perhaps class periods should be longer. By restricting lessons to 50 minutes, there simply is not enough time for students to truly immerse themselves within a task, activity, or assignment.

What's the evidence?

When combined, processing power and flow state suggest a very unique school day. Mornings would consist of six 30-minute class periods devoted to learning new material. Seeing as this would likely sap astrocytic glycogen stores, afternoons would then consist of a single 180-minute or two 90-minute class periods devoted to revising previously learned material, running extended lab sessions, or deeply engaging with ongoing projects. These extended lessons would encourage the emergence of flow, thereby allowing students to undertake deeply considered work.

Unfortunately, there has been no research into the impact of this cognitively aligned school day. Accordingly, it remains nothing more than a thought experiment.

With that said, some schools have embraced longer (90- or 120-minute) class periods through block scheduling. Although research suggests this can improve student/teacher relationships, the impact of block scheduling on general learning is varied: some schools show improvements while others show impairments. These mixed results suggest that what we're seeing is natural variation in learning with no real impact (good or bad) of block scheduling itself.

Far rarer, some schools have embraced shorter class periods. Unfortunately, although these schools claim better student motivation and learning, the research testing these claims is largely non-existent. This means the impact of this practice remains uncertain.

Though the historic function of the 50-minute class period had nothing to do with student learning, there is little solid evidence suggesting a more effective organization. But remember: absence of evidence is not the same as evidence of absence. Experiments with lesson length should certainly continue at the level of the individual school. Once enough evidence is accumulated from small-scale experiments, then we can make broader proclamations at district, state, and federal levels.

This leaves us with one last question – what about that odd school start time?

8 O'CLOCK BELL

Where did it come from?

International school start times differ significantly, ranging from 6 a.m. (Uganda) to 8:45 a.m. (UK) and even a little later. Despite this variation, one thing is consistent: the typical school day runs out of sync with the typical adult working day. Why is this?

The short answer is: nobody knows. So far as I can tell, there has never been a clear or explicit explanation put forward as to why school is organized in this way. With that said, there are several theories.

Perhaps the most popular argument for early school start times concerns traffic. More specifically, starting the school day before the working day cuts back on gridlock by ensuring school buses are off major roads before morning rush hour begins. Unfortunately, this explanation makes little sense when we consider that school start times in most Western countries have remained virtually unchanged since the 1800s, long before city traffic jams were an issue.

Another argument concerns sport. In order to ensure ample training time, schools must start early enough to allow athletes to harness afternoon sunlight. Though this might make sense in the US (where sport drives many educational decisions), it doesn't explain countries without organized school sports teams.

A final explanation concerns bus organization. Seeing as many schools can only afford a limited number of buses, school start times must be early enough to allow equal access (e.g. the same bus can be used to drop off primary students at 7 a.m. and then return to drop off high schoolers at 8 a.m. or vice versa). Again, I'm not certain this makes much sense, as many places do not stagger start times according to year levels.

In the end, the only conceivable reason I can discern for traditional school start times is 'because that's how it's always been done'. Seeing as this organizational feature was not selected to address any specific learning goals, it remains well and truly open for scrutiny.

Is it good for learning?

The relevant cognitive issue to consider here concerns <u>sleep-based memory consolidation</u>.

Human beings have a near 24-hour *circadian rhythm*; an internal clock that swings between wake and sleep. This rhythm means most people get tired around 8 p.m., are asleep around 10 p.m., and wake up around 6 a.m.

Interestingly, human beings do not sleep straight through the night. Rather, each night is typically divided into five 90-minute sleep cycles. During each of these cycles, the brain moves through 3 different stages of deep sleep.

During stage I, the brain rapidly transitions from wakefulness and reduces communication with the body. During stage II, the brain largely consolidates memories, essentially locking down new information and ideas encountered during the day. During stage III, the brain largely runs maintenance, essentially resetting and recharging (including refilling astrocytic glycogen stores) so it can tackle another day.

Importantly, we do not spend an equal amount of time in each stage of deep sleep. During the first 3 sleep cycles of the night, the brain spends most of its time in stage III sleep, cleaning itself out and recharging for the next day. It's not until the 4th and 5th sleep cycles of the night that the brain spends extended periods in stage II sleep, consolidating new memories.

Here's where things get fun.

During adolescence, the circadian rhythm shifts about 2 to 3 hours later (a process called *sleep phase delay*). This means many teenagers don't get tired until around 10:30 p.m., aren't asleep until around 12:30 a.m., and wouldn't naturally wake up until around 8:30 a.m. Unfortunately, despite this biological shift in sleep patterns, most teenagers must still wake up around 6 a.m. to attend school.

Do you see the issue?

If teens only sleep for 6 hours a night, they will only clear about 3.5 sleep cycles. This means that, although the brain will be ready to tackle the day, it will have spent only about 90 minutes consolidating memories and locking down newly learned information. If teens were able to get one additional sleep cycle per night, this would nearly double their total memory consolidation time.

What's the evidence?

Proponents of a later school start time argue that, with more time in stage II sleep, teenagers would demonstrate enhanced learning in the classroom. In fact, research largely supports this notion. Delaying school start time by one hour has been shown to generate not only small but significant increases in academic performance, but also increases in sleep duration (students don't simply stay up later), increases in wellbeing, decreases in absences, and decreases in tardiness.

This one looks cut and dry, right?

Not so fast.

Teenagers aren't the only stakeholders in education; we've also got younger students, teachers, and parents to consider. Taking into account extracurricular activities, a later school start time means some teachers would be stuck at school until 6 or 7 p.m. each night. Furthermore, so that parents aren't forced to make multiple school runs, delaying secondary school start time would likely mean delaying primary school start time as well. Unfortunately, younger students do not suffer from sleep phase delay, meaning there's no compelling learning argument to be made for them starting later.

In the end, the number of parties involved and logistics required to shift the morning bell might outweigh the considerations of teenage memory consolidation. Regardless, it's important that the final determination of school start time is made with clear and explicit reasoning: 'because that's the way we've always done it' is not a solid enough foundation upon which to base any important organizational decision.

SO NOW THEN…

In the end, many time-based organizing principles driving school are maintained out of habit, tradition, or routine. Although many people try to fight against these, routine is a like a moving train: difficult to stop once it's got momentum.

With that said, hopefully a recognition of the outdated functions behind certain organizational elements can help clarify the issues at stake and bring more focus to these ongoing debates. Unfortunately, there's certainly no single 'correct' answer to the questions of school organization. This means any decisions must ultimately be made by weighing many competing goals.

This raises one final, hugely important question: by what standard should we attempt to prioritize these goals? How do we determine which goals should be elevated to drive educational decisions?

This leads us to our final chapter. What, exactly, are schools aiming to achieve?

CHAPTER 10
PURPOSE – THE PROBLEM WITH NARRATIVE

"FORM FOLLOWS FUNCTION."
– LOUIS SULLIVAN

Though undoubtedly an oversimplification, it wouldn't be wrong to say that architecture (especially landmark architecture) has historically been driven by the motto *Form First*. In other words, practical utility has classically played second fiddle to aesthetic considerations. This is why it's not uncommon to hear people say of St Peter's Basilica, 'It's lovely, but I wouldn't want to attend Mass there,' or of Versailles, 'It's beautiful, but I wouldn't want to live there.'

Louis Sullivan was one of the first architects to buck this trend. Working in the late 19th century when skyscrapers were new and there was much debate over how best to design these unprecedented tall structures, Sullivan argued that it was time for architects to break with tradition and forge a new identity under the motto *Form Follows Function*. In other words, he believed that the practical utility should be of primary concern and drive all aesthetic decisions. This is the reason why skyscrapers the world over look the way they do: the hive-like layout reflects the easiest and most efficient way to balance the many competing needs that arise when massive commercial buildings are constructed on compact plots of land: needs like moving people through the building, circulating air within the building, and moving waste out of the building.

Lest you worry that using function to drive form can only ever produce ugly, utilitarian architecture (as many have accused skyscrapers of being), it's worth remembering that one of Sullivan's protégés was Frank Lloyd Wright – designer of some of the world's most beautiful and celebrated buildings. Rewording his teacher's motto to read *From Within, Outward*, Wright made it clear that beauty and style are crucially important; they simply must emerge from a deep, unambiguous deference to utility. Once it is clear how a space is to be used, then aesthetic decisions cannot help but elegantly reflect this.

A wonderful example of this philosophy is Wright's Guggenheim Art Museum in New York City. Wright built this structure, whose function is to publicly display works of art, as a single continuous ramp. Here, an undoubtedly beautiful structure springs directly from utility: patrons need only walk in a straight line to pass every single piece of art on display in the gallery. This is unlike the Louvre in Paris, which, although undeniably gorgeous, feels more like a maze and leaves visitors with the sense that they missed more art than they saw.

Why this seemingly irrelevant digression into architecture?

Most readers will recognize that the previous 9 chapters of this book have assumed a 'form first' mentality: What should we be teaching? How should we be organizing the day? Which tools should we be employing? In fact, educational discussion over the past six decades has almost exclusively been concerned with issues of form in the guise of how to teach most effectively.

Perhaps this is why debates among educators have been unceasing, academic crises have proved unsolvable, and fad cycles have become overbearing. When arguing about matters of structure, there is no ultimate benchmark against which to measure merit or determine success. Without a clear foundation upon which to base thinking and debate, form itself becomes a source of pride, and educators concern themselves with defending methods and techniques.

Although it's certainly worthwhile to debate the effectiveness of varied teaching methods, the ultimate and enduring question remains: effective for what?

Once we assume a 'form follows function' mentality, then we are forced to consider what precisely the function of school is. By this, I do not mean to question the function of education, which is a pervasive, lifelong, and ever-evolving endeavour. Rather, I mean to question the institution of school itself. What is the ultimate purpose of a structured K–12 and tertiary schooling system?

This is not an engineering question to be solved through technical measures; this is a metaphysical question to be solved through a deep consideration of purpose, intent, and meaning. This is not a question of *means*, but of *ends*. Only after the ultimate function of school has been made clear and explicit will we ever be able to make meaningful decisions concerning form.

This is why it's exceedingly rare to hear about educational crises or teacher strife within military academies, art institutes, or fundamentalist religious schools.

These institutions embody an unambiguous function, and the type of human being each aims to forge is never in doubt. Educators in these schools almost certainly debate pedagogical strategies – but, with a clear function upon which to base decision-making, these debates take on the flavour of experimentation and evolution rather than rebellion and revolution.

So, what is the function of school?

NARRATIVE

Paraphrasing educator Neil Postman, public schools do not exist to *serve* a public; they exist to *create* a public. Importantly, the answer as to what kind of public they are creating won't be found in the teaching methods employed, the homework assigned, or the uniforms worn. The answer will be found in the story used (knowingly or unknowingly) to imbue the entire endeavour with meaning.

In other words, the function of schooling is best identified by the Narrative that this institution serves. Here, I don't mean lower-case *n* narrative that takes the form of a vision statement or motto. I mean upper-case N Narrative that takes the form of an all-encompassing description of the world. Think Catholicism, Marxism, or Evolutionary Psychology. These Narratives do not merely enlighten; they supply the very meaning that sustains, guides, and propels adherents forward.

With such a hefty responsibility, an effective Narrative cannot simply be any old story. Instead, it must meet three key criteria:

1) Continuity

   A Narrative organizes the past, present, and future into a coherent and consistent framework. It answers the question of how things came to be, which in turn gives clarity to the current state of the world and offers guidance as to how affairs can (and should) evolve.

2) Personal Identity

   A Narrative makes clear the role of individual human beings in the prior and continuing evolution of the world. It outlines the elements of a 'righteous life' and supplies the paragon against which personal identity can be defined and established.

3) Social Organization

> A Narrative arranges broader public affairs in a manner that privileges communal ideals. It establishes basic tenets of 'civilized' behaviour within the social sphere, and esteems collective principles that transcend the individual self.

As an example, let's consider education at the birth of the United States. Spearheaded largely by Thomas Jefferson, public schooling in post-revolutionary America was established under a very specific and unambiguous Narrative: *the Democratic Experiment.*

Through this Narrative, history is understood as a series of struggles to maintain personal liberty in the face of increasingly tyrannical power structures. In other words, leaders left unchecked have always preyed upon the fundamental rights of their flock (*continuity*). Armed with this knowledge, students must recognize that they are inherently free individuals tasked with protecting and maintaining that freedom through the vigilant surveillance of emerging power structures. In other words, a virtuous life is marked by knowing why, when, and how to defend personal liberty against tyrants (*identity*). Thus empowered, students will embrace civic duties that safeguard the means of all citizens to check and balance the authority of power structures in all guises. In other words, citizens will develop essential norms, mores, and protocols that champion the ideal 'all men are created equal' (*social organization*).

From the outset, Jefferson made clear the function of education. As he unequivocally put it, 'public schooling is the keystone in the arch of our government.'

Although the Democratic Experiment Narrative is incredibly powerful and deeply sustaining, there's no question that it has long since faded. The idea of organizing history according to varying degrees of oppression still echoes throughout much modern political thought, but few people continue to believe that the function of public schooling is to churn out revolutionaries in the mould of Thomas Jefferson. Furthermore, it becomes abundantly clear that civic participation is no longer a driving force behind personal or collective identity in the US when you learn that nearly 50% of eligible voters did not cast a ballot in the last major election or that nearly 70% of Americans cannot name any current state representative.

Here's the rub: like nature, Narrative abhors a vacuum. When a story dies, the void left behind does not stay empty for long. Very quickly, a new story will rush in and establish a new function. This can be problematic as, without careful forethought and consideration, the new Narrative will likely be one that few people asked for, few people appreciate, and few people are even consciously aware of.

This is exactly what has happened to modern schooling in the West (and, one supposes, much of the East). A contemporary Narrative has risen and established a function that influences nearly every governmental and leadership decision. Unfortunately, most educators are unaware of (or underestimate) the immense gravity of what has occurred.

ECONOMIC CONSUMERS

The Narrative driving modern schooling can be dubbed *Genesis of the Economic Consumer*. This Narrative has two primary maxims:

I. You are what you do for a living.

II. Worth is measured according to the goods you possess.

As alluded to in Chapter 3, if you ask 100 *non*-educators what the function of school is, there's a good chance the majority will provide an answer that reflects these two maxims. To the world at large, K–12 and tertiary schooling serves to prepare students for the workforce, which in turn will allow them to contribute to the national economy by purchasing goods and services.

Whether you love or loathe these maxims is irrelevant; this Narrative persists because it effectively meets all three essential criteria:

- It offers *continuity* by organizing history into a series of increasingly complex interactions based on the goods produced and traded amongst various groups. This, in turn, serves to clarify the present and guide the future according to market forces.

- It constructs *personal identity* by causing students to identify themselves as economic units tasked with achieving the 'good life' as measured by salary (such that a higher salary signifies more meaningful work). Self-worth, subsequently, is defined according to human capital: those skills, competencies, and knowledge one acquires throughout life that make him/her better suited for high-earning employment.

- It drives *social organization* according to wealth classes, and ensures personal earnings are meaningful only inasmuch as they're used to purchase goods and services from others (thereby enabling all citizens to contribute to collective wealth). Ultimately, the growth of a nation's economy takes precedence – by improving the whole, we improve the individual.

Here's the problem: if you ask 100 educators what the function of school is, there's a high probability that none will provide an answer that reflects this Narrative. It's not that teachers are indifferent to employment or career paths; it's simply that these issues rarely embody the primary passions that lead one to become a teacher. In fact, most educators will report that the function of schooling is something along the following lines: to create happy, healthy, holistic life-long learners receptive to diverse viewpoints, capable of questioning standards, and willing to adapt personal opinion. School serves to build a confident and creative society capable not only of successfully navigating the world as it is, but also of changing it for the better.

So, how is it possible that the Economic Consumer Narrative has survived for decades when most practitioners neither endorse nor particularly care for it?

Look again at that traditional educator vision outlined above: those attributes teachers strive for (tolerance, confidence, open-mindedness) are non-specific ideals that do not cohere into a clear Narrative. This collection of traits says nothing about how the pieces of the world fit together, it doesn't outline a moral or ethical structure against which to construct an identity, and it fails to clarify the function of social norms in establishing collective aspirations. Put simply, it doesn't carry enough weight to effectively push back against the prevailing Narrative.

Don't get me wrong – I am not arguing against these traits. As an educator, I work every day to empower my students with a sense of confidence and capability. However, the ultimate question of function remains. *For what purpose* are students developing confidence and capability? *To what end* are they learning to be adaptable and open-minded? Without a clear function, the ceaseless and largely depleting debate over form will continue to rage unchecked.

Luckily, we are not beholden to the Economic Consumer Narrative. Though it is certainly effective, there are three glaring cracks in its façade that leave it vulnerable to rejection and replacement.

The first crack concerns sustenance. When 'making a living' becomes synonymous with 'making a life', many students tune out and begin searching for a Narrative that provides deeper meaning. Perhaps this is why fewer than 50% of students report feeling engaged with school, and why the number of families pursuing alternative schooling increases by about 5% every year. Currently, these trends are being debated from an engineering standpoint. (Can we increase engagement by decreasing class size? Will students stay if we implement project-based learning?) However, it's more likely that they reflect a problem of psyche precipitated by an unfulfilling Narrative.

The second crack concerns curricula. Those research projects that quantitatively analyse teaching techniques (Visible Learning, High Reliability Schools, etc.) have by and large concluded that music, exercise, and dramatic arts programmes do little to advance academic achievement. These findings have, in turn, led many schools to abandon these programmes and, instead, focus only on those fields relevant to the current job market. Oddly, proponents of the arts and athletics have often combatted this shift by trying to prove their fields can, in fact, boost employability: they have moved away from the ideal of 'art for art's sake' and embraced art as a way to boost numeracy, literacy, and other human capital skills. While it may be true that playing sport can boost academic outcomes, this argument serves only to embrace an Economic Consumer Narrative that runs antithetically to the broader values of health, teamwork, and creative expression that have historically driven these fields.

The third crack concerns validity. If the Economic Consumer Narrative was well founded, then one would reasonably expect to see a strong positive correlation between a country's academic outcomes and its economy. Although this relationship appears to exist amongst low-income countries at or below $20,000 gross domestic product per capita, such a correlation is absent among countries that surpass this threshold. In fact, of the world's 10 largest economies, only two ranked amongst the Top 10 in maths performance (China and Japan) and reading performance (China and Canada) according to the most recent international PISA results.

Indeed, the Economic Consumer Narrative is weakened by evident (and increasingly urgent) shortcomings that make it susceptible to replacement. This begs the question: what counter-Narratives exist that might realistically mount a challenge while simultaneously elevating educational discourse and imbuing school with a more fulfilling function?

Below I outline three, but please do not take these to be comprehensive. There are dozens of viable Narratives ripe for discussion and potential adoption.

ALTERNATIVE NARRATIVES

Planetary Stewards

Let us be good stewards of the Earth we inherited... If we are to go on living together on this Earth, we must all be responsible for it.
Kofi Annan

During the summer of 2019/2020, Australia suffered through one of the most devastating bush fire seasons on record. In just 4 months, over 18 million hectares of land burned, over 9 thousand homes and businesses were destroyed, and over 1 billion local animals were killed. Needless to say, when students returned to school following the summer break, the world was no longer the same for many of them. This fact hit home for me personally when, before storming out of class, one of my students turned to me and asked, 'Why do I need to get a degree when there won't even be a planet for me to practise that degree on?'

Between protests, sit-ins, and strikes, students the world over have spent the last decade clamouring for a better school Narrative; and they've not hidden which particular Narrative they feel is most important. Climate change is forcing us to re-evaluate nearly every human endeavour, and is quickly becoming a primary driver of public discourse. So, what are the maxims of Planetary Stewardship?

I.   The Earth is not eternal and, like all things, will some day die.

II. Human action serves to either accelerate or delay this process.

III. Enduring survival mandates a relationship of mutual beneficence and growth between humanity and our home.

This Narrative organizes the past according to interactions between humanity and Earth, with the defining characteristic being the impact these interactions have had on the health and sustainability of the planet and its inhabitants. This historical continuity greatly clarifies issues of the modern world and helps paint a picture of how the future can (and should) play out.

From this, a moral compass is constructed around the premise that every action has consequences. Tasked with Stewardship, identity develops according to a recognition and refinement of behaviour in support of a personal equilibrium with the environment. Beyond this, the collective ideal of maintaining and improving the planet for future generations becomes paramount. It's not enough to merely change personal behaviours; we must ensure proper social structures and norms are established that enable all people to change behaviours (such as organically grown foods not being priced beyond the means of average consumers).

In addition to being incredibly fulfilling, this Narrative would prove powerful within schools because it neither constricts nor dictates curricula. Seeing as all actions reflect the basic humanity–environment relationship, Stewardship can serve to provide fundamental meaning to any and every field of academic study. In addition, this Narrative presents the world as dynamically evolving, which fosters a sense of openness and invites everyone to leverage their respective passions to contribute to collective betterment.

<u>Giant Climbers</u>

> *If I have seen further it is by standing on the shoulders of Giants.*
>
> **Isaac Newton**

History is a veritable graveyard of once promising theories that were discarded in the face of evolving knowledge and thought. But knowledge and thought can only ever evolve through a conscious deference to those abandoned theories of the past.

Once this virtuous cycle is recognized, then it becomes clear that the theories we hold as gospel today will also change – and herein lies the Narrative of the Giant Climbers. The maxims of this story include:

I. No idea is everlasting: knowledge is transitory and will always evolve.

II. Each generation is tasked with pushing beyond the ideas of the past, which requires a deep and nuanced understanding of those ideas and their genesis.

III. The new ideas we establish today will dictate the starting point for the next generation.

This Narrative organizes the past according to a progression of theories, including the social, environmental, and psychological contexts that shaped this progression. History, then, is marked by stretches of stasis (when people fought to maintain ideas in the face of contrary evidence) punctuated by periods of change (when a new idea bubbled forth and altered everything). Organizing the world in this way not only provides a solid foundation for modern conceptions of the world, but also indicates that these conceptions are not final.

From this, a moral compass is constructed around an awareness of and tolerance for past and present thinkers, as well as a duty to engage in meaningful personal thought. Tasked with Giant Climbing, identity builds according to the practice of confronting, understanding, and pushing back against norms and structures put in place by those who lacked modern perspective. Importantly, this gives rise to the larger ideals of intellectual liberty and cognitive collectivism. All ideas supported by deep knowledge of the past are viable, while collective utility is ultimately determined by social diffusion and acceptance.

As before, this Narrative would prove particularly powerful within schools, as it does not discriminate. Every single field – from woodworking to calculus – has a history of ideas that can be drawn upon to provide clarity and purpose to current learning. In addition, this Narrative empowers to the degree that it does not cling tightly to notions of Truth, and encourages everyone to contribute to the world of ideas through learning, deep comprehension, and meaningful thought. In the words of Walt Whitman: 'That the powerful play goes on, and you may contribute a verse.'

Toolmakers

> *Without tools [humanity] is nothing, with tools [it] is all.*
> **Thomas Carlyle**

Though many animals employ devices in their daily routines, only human beings have come to define their existence according to tools. Nearly everything we interact with – from chairs to contact lenses to this very book you're reading now – is an unnatural construct cut from the mind of humanity. Importantly, as we explored in Chapter 3, tools are far from inert and each serves to shape our perceptions, our psychologies, and our societies.

This means that tools themselves can form the basis of an organizing Narrative. When technology becomes the object of inquiry, and not merely the means through which to undertake inquiry, then we can develop a new way of understanding and engaging with the 'world of things' around us. The maxims of this Narrative include:

I. Humanity makes tools. Thereupon, tools make humanity.

II. Human evolution can be understood through the tools created and utilized.

III. The future of humanity will be written by the tools we invent and collectively choose to employ.

This Narrative organizes the past according to development. It not only delineates the most important tools invented throughout history, but also ponders the conditions that necessitated the creation of each and, more importantly, seeks to understand how each changed our thinking about the world, its function, and our place within it. Modern tools and contemporary worldviews consequently open themselves up to examination. Ultimately, a vision of the future can be rationally constructed alongside a judicious understanding of how tools should (and should not) be used to support this vision.

From this, a moral compass is built around the obligation to decouple intentions from implements. Tasked with toolmaking, identity builds according to our capacity to evaluate the long-term impact of emerging technologies and create tools which support (rather than dictate) personal drives. Tellingly, often the only reliable way to discern the full impact of a tool is to witness how it alters social norms and organization. This means collective behaviours must be elevated above personal experience and private interests when determining the ultimate utility of emerging technologies.

Again, seeing as tools exert influence over every aspect of our physical and mental lives, this Narrative does not dictate curricula and can be used to support all subjects and fields of study. In addition, this Narrative strongly delineates between the 'natural' and the 'human-made', which can serve as a powerful foundation for personal exploration and self-actualization. Finally, it's possible that combining the Toolmaking and Planetary Stewardship Narratives will force us to extend considerations beyond human beings and consider how tools impact the Earth itself.

SO NOW THEN...

Take notice the next time a student asks, 'Why do I need to learn this?' The answer we collectively supply (as teachers, administrators, and parents) reflects the true function of modern schooling.

Today, the most consistent answer is, 'Because it will help you pass exams, get into a good university, secure a good job, and earn enough money to provide for your children. You want to give your future kids the best opportunities in life, don't you?'

It is difficult to fault the insidious decisions of form that many schools make in the name of this particular function, such as ability streaming, selective enrolment, high-stakes summative exams, abandoning electives, and punitive behavioural management. Though these practices may not reflect the true goals and passions of practising teachers, they perfectly serve the Economic Consumer Narrative.

The fact that people around the world are pushing back against these practices suggests that we collectively recognize something is amiss. Unfortunately, many are taking aim at the wrong targets: 'Let's decrease school hours, increase play-based learning, and supply healthy lunches.' Although these are virtuous objectives, the true source of academic disillusionment does not spring from issues of engineering.

It's time to switch our aim back to purpose. It's time to reassess the meaning of school. It's time to move beyond generic calls for confidence, creativity, and critical thinking, and instead consider what Narrative we wish to define schools into the future.

The next time a student asks, 'Why do I need to learn this?', what answer would make us proud?

Form follows function.

OUTRO

Education is not broken.

But the world is changing.

When we stand still, we go backwards. Tradition and historical practices matter – but they should act as a stabilising keel rather than a rusty anchor. Education doesn't need an external revolution; it merely needs continuous internal evolution. Educators need not look outside of the craft for answers; they need only turn inwards and learn from the collective expertise born from millions of hours at the chalkface.

As Arthur Schopenhauer said:

> The task is not so much to see what no one has yet seen; but to think what nobody has yet thought concerning that which everybody sees.

To move education forward, our job is not to see something new. Our job is to think deeply, openly, and expertly about those aspects of school that every student, teacher, leader, and parent can already clearly see.

Which begs the question: if we've seen it all, why does a book like this matter? As the old adage says, 'You can't read the label while you're sitting inside the jar.' Often, we are so deep inside our own work that it becomes difficult to gain new perspective and cultivate the space necessary to 'think what nobody has yet thought'.

This is the function that external experts and books like this can serve; they can offer a meaningful, contemplative, forward-feeding process that enables us to step outside the jar.

Even so, once we're outside the jar and the label becomes visible, all we can see are the ingredients. But those mouth-watering pies your grandmother bakes and those perfect dumplings your favourite restaurant serves – they require more than ingredients. They require deep knowledge that can only be developed through explicit practice. This is where expertise comes to the fore.

As we established in Chapter 1, teachers are the only people in the world who devote the time, effort, and energy required to develop expertise in teaching. Moreover, as we discussed in Chapter 2, emergent properties within a classroom can only ever be accounted for inside the classroom. This suggests that teachers are the only ones poised to meaningfully translate the 'ingredients' explored throughout this book for the sake of driving educational change.

Unfortunately, if this book has awakened a sense of possibility or sparked an idea, you're about to face a significant obstacle: educational inertia.

There is arguably no field in the world with a stronger immune system than education. This is understandable: when seemingly everyone is shouting for reforms that suit only their immediate aims, putting up a strong defence and hunkering down is not an unreasonable response. But alas, this inertia means modern education is deeply entrenched and notoriously difficult to change. If you have any appetite for innovation, you are sure to come up against a seemingly impenetrable 'system'.

Luckily, there is a potential solution.

During World War II, the United States War Department needed to quickly develop faster, more agile planes that could compete with the powerful German Luftwaffe. Unfortunately, the aeronautic 'system' was deeply entrenched and committed to propeller technology. This created a stiff bureaucracy bent on impeding any experimentation with emerging jet technology.

Developers were forced to step outside the jar.

Lockheed Aircraft Corporation circumvented this bureaucracy by setting up a small circus tent away from their main production facility. This tent, which was erected next to a horribly malodorous plastics factory, was dubbed Skunk Works.

Inside Skunk Works, a small group of 53 engineers and mechanics was given free rein to experiment. Their only imperative was to build a fighter plane that would tilt the aerial advantage in favour of the Allies. Because personnel and funding were limited, this group could innovate in a manner that neither threatened the larger aeronautic 'system' nor strained Lockheed itself. Skunk Works was able to test assumptions, fail without repercussion, and iterate freely until, only 143 days into the project, they delivered the XP-80: the world's first jet fighter capable of flying over 250 kilometres per hour faster than the propeller-driven Mustang and Spitfire planes.

The success of Lockheed's Skunk Works has led many companies to emulate this concept, from tech upstarts like Google and Apple to rooted blue-chips like Walmart and Ford. While each Skunk Works is unique, they are all based on the same philosophy: evolve the system by experimenting, failing, and iterating at the fringe – because this is the least risky place for innovations to mature before they are integrated into the mainstream.

Importantly, these groups do not threaten the larger 'system'. If 10 people working in isolation develop an effective model, only then is it step-wise introduced and tested across the larger office, district, and company. If, however, those same 10 people fail, the broader impact is nominal.

Believe it or not, in an academic setting, this liminal fringe exists within the classroom. As you read these words, thousands of Skunk Works are happening behind closed classroom doors across the globe. Every day, teachers with an unimaginable quantity of collective expertise are working on the educational equivalent of the XP-80. The only pieces they lack are a standard means of documenting their work, an open source to disseminate their work, and a sponsored system to scale their successes across more classrooms.

And herein lies the promise of a body of knowledge. Imagine what will happen if we afford teachers the time, space, and incentive to develop their ideas by undertaking strategic experimentation in the classroom.

Like all forms of evolution, much of this work is unlikely to go anywhere – but this won't materially impact the larger school or educational ecosystem. Occasionally, however, strategies will emerge that will be worth testing across other classes, schools, and districts. Embracing a Skunk Works mentality will drive grassroots change while obviating the need for radical top-down overhaul.

The ultimate goal should not be revolution driven by external interests – it should be evolution driven by those who possess the knowledge, skill, and expertise to properly drive it: teachers themselves.

References and Resources (link)

For a complete list of the references and resources that have informed this book, please visit:

www.10thingsbook.com/references